The Real Common Worship

CW01025036

The Real Common Worship

edited by Peter Mullen

Edgeways

first published November 2000
by Edgeways Books
an imprint of The Brynmill Press Ltd
Pockthorpe Cottage, Denton, Nr Harleston,
Norfolk. IP20 0AS

and printed by Antony Rowe Ltd, Bumper's Farm,
Chippenham, Wiltshire. SN14 6LH

ISBN 0 907839 64 9 (hard covers)
ISBN 0 907839 67 3 (paper covers)

copyright © contributors 2000
typography copyright © The Brynmill Press Ltd 2000

British Library Cataloguing in Publication Data: A Catalogue record of this book is available from the British Library.

Acknowledgements

Text from the booklet, *Common Worship: Planning for Change* (Church House Publishing) is copyright © The Archbishops' Council, 2000 and is reproduced by permission.

"The Prayer Book and Our English i" is the Introduction to the Everyman's Library Edition of the Book of Common Prayer, 1999, and is reprinted by kind permission of the author and David Campbell Publishers Ltd.

"The Prayer Book and Our English ii", the address at the presentation of The Thomas Cranmer Schools Prize at St James Garlickhythe, 19 December 1989, was published in *The Daily Mail* the following day, and has been reprinted in a Prayer Book Society pamphlet and in *The People's Prince: a Collection of Major Addresses*, Perth, Western Australia, 1992.

The first version of "Common Prayer and the Pirates" was a paper delivered to and published by the Manchester branch of the Prayer Book Society, November, 1997, slightly modified and published in *Faith and Worship* 44, Summer 1998.

"The Question of Style" includes material from the following contributions to *Faith and Worship*: "Long Live the Prayer Book Blessings", 38, Summer, 1995; "A Considerable Body of New Prayer Material", 44, Summer, 1998; and "Oh! O Commissioners", 48, Summer 2000.

Contents

Preface

The latest stage in the Church of England's programme of liturgical reform, which began in 1928 with the revised Book of Common Prayer, is reached in Autumn 2000 with the publication of Common Worship. This provides an occasion to examine the recent history of the Church's altered services. How has the programme of liturgical revision been received by worshipping congregations over recent decades? We have included some conjectures on the subject, based on statistics of church attendance.

Some will be surprised that a new service book was thought necessary a mere twenty years after the publication of The Alternative Service Book, 1980. The Liturgical Commission has explained this necessity. "The task of liturgy is to create resonances with people's experience and to identify with people where they are." In other words, the Commission judges the public to have different experiences from those of 1980 and to be in a different place.

Literature needs criticism, and this is true of liturgical literature. The Liturgical Commission implicitly accepts this principle, for they give as one of the reasons necessitating a new book that "Some parts of the ASB have proved to be weaker than others."

On the same principle, if the Alternative Service Book was thought necessary in 1980, that must have been because the Book of Common Prayer was then regarded as unsatisfactory, at least in part. We try, by critical comparison and theological and literary examination of the texts, to determine whether previous rites and ceremonies have in fact been improved upon in Common Worship. Political and social changes as well as developments in spoken and written English—what Thomas Cranmer referred to as "evident necessities"—over a long period of time might well create the need for a new Prayer Book. We ask whether there are such evident necessities.

Of course, the Liturgical Commission has decided views on all these related issues, and to report them accurately we have included their own explanation of the need for Common Worship.

In discussions about liturgies it is sometimes said that people should not "get bogged down in mere words". Unfortunately, the choice of words determines what is being said; and that is why the utmost care must be taken over the words used. If this is true for ordinary communications and the "arts" of prose and poetry, how much the more it must hold for the creation of the language of worship! Style is therefore discussed here, but not as if it were mere ornament. *How* something is said is in the end inseparable from *what* is being said. So in liturgy there is the closest connection between style and theology. The supreme work of liturgy is the mediation of the sacred, and so we have to ask how successfully this is achieved in the Book of Common Prayer and in Common Worship.

How the nation prays and worships reveals the religious and spiritual character of the nation; so in a final chapter we have tried to describe how liturgical changes fit in with many of the other features of the way we live now. About that, though our contributors write for themselves, the whole book forms a judgement.

I
The Prayer Book and Our English
i

This essay forms the Introduction to the Everyman's Library edition of The Book of Common Prayer, 1999.

Diarmaid MacCulloch

The Book of Common Prayer is one of the most important books in the English language. This is not because it is an incomparable road to heaven (though some still find it to be), nor even because it remains in formal terms the standard liturgy through which the established Church of England leads a nation in worshipping God. Rather, it is important as one of a handful of texts to have decided the future of a world language. These key texts emerged in a small northern-European kingdom in the sixteenth century, and they are threefold: beside the Prayer Book, masterminded by Thomas Cranmer (1489–1556), they consist of the Bible as translated from Hebrew, Greek and Latin by William Tyndale (*c.* 1490–1536) and Miles Coverdale (1488–1568), and the plays of William Shakespeare

(1564–1616). Together, these have shaped sound patterns and speech structures through which billions of the human race communicate with each other.

Among these three sources of world English, the Prayer Book has a unique place, because it is a piece of theatre designed to be performed by an entire people, week by week, day by day. Tyndale's Bible is intended to be read by the faithful, or to be listened to at home or in church. Shakespeare's plays allow a company of actors to act out before an audience the triumphs, the comedy and tragedy of human life. The Prayer Book has all these purposes and intentions, yet it combines them in a drama of human life and destiny where all those present have a speaking part. "The Lord be with you" is the greeting from the leader of worship at Morning and Evening Prayer, and since the year 1549 back has come the greeting response from the people, "And with thy spirit." "Lift up your hearts," says the priest as the drama of Holy Communion gathers pace: "We lift them up unto the Lord" is the reply. For several centuries, the people in church admittedly had a cheerleader or spokesman in the performance, the parish clerk. In many ancient English parish churches there are pulpits in three decks for parson and clerk: the parson sat in his deck above the clerk, in the Prayer Book dialogue of God's service, before he climbed up to the third pulpit deck to take the worship further in his sermon. The sermon would be an exploration of the English biblical text which Tyndale pioneered, and which was read in sequence throughout the Prayer Book's year.

The Prayer Book in History

To understand why this book was created, we go back to the sixteenth century. In 1500 all Europe, as far east as what are now the Baltic states, Poland, Slovakia, Hungary and Croatia, was united by a single culture and by a single branch of the Christian Church. It was led by those who spoke Latin as their natural language, and by one symbolic head, the Bishop of Rome (the Pope). Over the century, this western Latin church fell apart in a complex sequence of bitter ideological battles, which we call the Reformation. The Reformation upheavals represented the greatest fault-line to appear in Christian culture since the Latin and Greek halves of the Roman Empire had gone their separate ways a thousand years earlier. The cause was a deep disagreement about how human beings could be saved to eternal life, how they might exercise the saving power of God in the world—arguments even about what it was to be human. Ranged on one side were traditional Church leaders who stressed the authority of their institution, and its power to create the body and blood of God out of bread and wine, in the eucharistic service known as the Mass. Lined up against them was a great variety of protestors (many of them also clergy) who saw these claims as bogus. They said that a great many beliefs and doctrines proclaimed by the western Church were distortions of true Christianity as seen in the Bible, and that the Church authorities had sought to usurp God's power. They regarded the Mass used by the Roman Church as the centrepiece of a huge confidence trick. Because of one very specific political protest made in 1529 by a group of German princes, the challengers came to be known as Protestants.

One central Protestant aim was to give back to ordinary people their full part in worship. The medieval western Church had maintained the use of Latin for the liturgy. Latin had been the universal language of the western

Roman Empire, and it was still understood and regularly used in everyday life by educated people; however, it could be seen as excluding or marginalizing the large majority of Europeans who were not educated. So in England the coming of the Reformation brought a liturgy in English, the Book of Common Prayer. It was not called "Common Prayer" for nothing: it was meant to be prayer shared in common. In areas of the Tudor realms which spoke a different language, the book was translated accordingly: French for the Channel Isles, Welsh for Wales, and (disastrously belated), Gaelic for the Gaelic-speaking parts of Ireland. It could even be used in Latin where Latin was the normal language: Oxford and Cambridge colleges and some major schools like Eton.

In England, the Reformation was begun in the reign of Henry VIII (1509–47), when the King was blocked by the Pope in his efforts to have his marriage to Queen Catherine of Aragon declared null and void. Pious, intensely egocentric and opinionated, Henry became convinced that the Pope's obstinacy was a devilish conspiracy against God's wish that the King should get what he wanted. So he broke with Rome, just at the moment when a significant faction among his clergy were becoming excited by the Reformation's explosion of religious energy on the Continent. Henry chose one of these clergy, a diplomat and Cambridge don called Thomas Cranmer, to be his Archbishop of Canterbury, because he liked and trusted Cranmer and knew that he was determined to see through the annulment of the Aragon marriage.

Thus Cranmer came to the highest position in the church, with his own agenda for religious revolution, which did not always coincide with the King's eccentric mixture of religious beliefs. Two of his chief priorities were to see the Bible published in English, and the worship of the Church changed from Latin to English. With the powerful help of Cranmer's friend and collaborator, the King's chief minister Thomas Cromwell, a version of Tyndale's and Coverdale's English Bible translation was legalized, and then a further revision of it was given official status (the so-called "Great Bible") in 1539. At the same time, Cranmer started reshaping the Latin services of the medieval Church into English. Henry was not enthusiastic for the idea, and so while the old King lived, the only part of this work to be made public and official was the Litany, the solemn recitation of prayers in dialogue by priest and people, usually walking in procession. This is substantially still the Litany to be found in the Prayer Book.

When Henry's young son became King Edward VI in 1547, government fell into the hands of a group of Protestant noblemen who were Cranmer's close colleagues. Now he could make much more progress with his plans. In particular, he had come to radical conclusions about the Church's central act of worship, the Eucharist. Along with many Protestant reformers (the main exception being the rather conservative Martin Luther), he no longer believed that bread and wine could turn physically into the body and blood of Christ on every eucharistic table in Christendom. Christ's body was in heaven at the right hand of God, and it was blasphemous to suppose that he could be elsewhere. Accordingly, for Cranmer, what happened in the Eucharist was that Christ called believers up to him in heaven, rather than coming down to them himself in bodily form into bread and wine. If he was present in the service, it was in spiritual form, a gift provided only for those faithful whom

God had chosen. People who were damned would have no experience of his presence, even if they were attending Communion. It is this "spiritual presence" view of the Eucharist which underpinned Cranmer's remodelling of the Prayer Book.

The Archbishop's changes were slowed up only by the need to conciliate still-powerful religious conservatives, and to avoid too much trouble with the large proportion of Edward's subjects who were bewildered by religious change. Accordingly, he introduced his work in stages. First, in 1548, he created "an Order of Communion", an English rite to be inserted in the old Latin Mass, so that at every Eucharist the people were exhorted to come forward and then received the consecrated bread and wine (over the previous five centuries, most laypeople had communicated as infrequently as once a year, and even then, only received the bread). This Order is still substantially embedded in the text of the Communion Service. Then in 1549 came the first version of the Prayer Book, the entire liturgy presented in English.

In order to get the reluctant consent of conservative politicians, the book was not a wholehearted break with the past. In the justifications for change given in its preface (the section of the book now headed "Concerning the Service of the Church"), the emphasis was on the complexity of the old services, the confused way in which they presented the text of scripture, and the variety of service patterns ("uses") even within the single kingdom of England. "From henceforth all the whole Realm shall have but one Use." Besides drawing heavily on the liturgies created by Protestant reformers in Europe, Cranmer adapted the medieval use customary at Salisbury Cathedral and which had become widely popular in England, the "Sarum Use". His theme of uniformity was taken up a few years later by the Roman Catholic Church (that part of the old western Church which remained loyal to the Pope): at the Council of Trent, it created a single eucharistic rite for the whole Roman Church, the Tridentine Mass, as the centrepiece of a whole range of standardized services.

Cranmer's new book attracted mixed reactions. In Devon and Cornwall in 1549, popular anger about it became full-scale rebellion, which the government brutally repressed; the rebels famously called the new Communion service "a Christmas game" because it was in English. However, in eastern and southern England, where there were widespread popular disturbances over a variety of other grievances, the protestors gladly used the new Prayer Book. Thereafter, Cranmer and King Edward's government were emboldened to go further. Cranmer was annoyed that more subtle conservatives, in particular his long-standing rival Stephen Gardiner the Bishop of Winchester, were saying that the 1549 Prayer Book was perfectly capable of being used just like the old services, and could be understood as expressing the old theology; this was not at all what Cranmer had intended. Accordingly, by 1552 he had drastically revised the book to express his ideas more emphatically. The changes are most obvious in the Communion Service, when compared with that of 1549. Even the title of the service has changed. In 1549, three different theological identities were on offer: "The Supper of the Lord and the Holy Communion, commonly called the Mass". Now even that last very grudging inclusion of the traditional name "Mass" was suppressed, and the service restructured to remove any idea that the bread and wine could be identified with the physical body and blood of Christ. The shape of this service remains essentially intact, although the 1662 revision of the book made small modifications, designed to make it possible to hold a more positive view of how the bread and wine showed forth the presence of God.

Equally revolutionary was Cranmer's 1552 restructuring of his 1549 Funeral Service. One of the great issues of the Reformation was the power which the old Church claimed to exercise over death and the departed. Medieval theology saw three possibilities for the human soul after death; in a few cases of exceptional sanctity, the soul might be ready for heaven, while for the truly wicked, there was no doubt that hell beckoned, but for most humans, neither especially bad nor especially good, the likely fate was a time of purging, punishment and refining, in a state known as purgatory. The attraction of the doctrine of purgatory was that it gave hope to humanity: purgatory was a prelude to heaven, and therefore a chance for ordinary fallible people to achieve eternal bliss. Moreover, the old Church increasingly maintained that it was possible to lessen one's time in purgatory by doing good works in earthly life, among which were prayers, especially the powerful prayer of the Mass. The living could also pray for the dead in purgatory, and thus do good to both parties. In some sense, the living could influence the fate of the dead. It was a compelling idea which the reformers, Cranmer among them, detested and were determined to combat.

The old Funeral Service therefore needed drastic revision in order to remove the idea that performing it might help the dead in any way. In the halfway-house book of 1549 there were still traces of the old ethos—psalms to recite, a direct address by the priest to the corpse, the possibility of celebrating a Eucharist as part of the funeral—but in 1552 all that changed. The historian Eamon Duffy comments that "the oddest feature of the 1552 rite is the disappearance of the corpse from it ... at the moment of committal in 1552, the minister turns not towards the corpse, but away from it, to the living congregation around the grave."[1] The Church in England thus surrendered its power over death back to the Lord of life and death in heaven: it was a move of perfect theological consistency in Cranmer's terms, but one which also rather sidestepped the problem of whether or not the deceased had been chosen by God for salvation. It has ceased to satisfy the pastoral needs of modern Anglicanism.

Cranmer's 1552 book was used for less than a year before young King Edward died (probably of pneumonia); his Catholic half-sister Mary restored the entire old Church and imprisoned Archbishop Cranmer on charges of treason and heresy. Probably if Edward had lived, Cranmer would have changed the Prayer Book still further. Instead he was burned at the stake, a hesitant, reluctant but ultimately an heroic martyr for the Reformation in England. Mary's reign lasted a mere five years (cancer, not pneumonia, this time), and the final long-lived Tudor, Elizabeth I, brought back a Protestant Church—with it, Cranmer's Prayer Book, hardly altered. With further modifications, made in 1662 when the episcopal Church of England had been recreated after Charles II had returned from civil war exile, the book achieved its final form. It was accompanied by a doctrinal statement lightly revised by Elizabeth's bishops from a production of Edward's reign: the Thirty-Nine Articles, still

[1] E. Duffy, *The Stripping of the Altars: Traditional Religion in England 1400–1580*, New Haven, 1992, pp. 473–5.

recognized as an essential part of the Church's historic inheritance.

The Prayer Book remained the only legal form of worship in the established churches of England, Wales and Ireland down to the twentieth century, when in common with all the churches of the west, extensive experiments with new liturgies began. The Alternative Service Book of the Church of England still proclaims by its name that the Prayer Book remains the standard by which all the Church's worship is to be judged. Nevertheless, when this new book was first introduced in 1980, it announced a very modern guiding principle that "revision and adaptation of the church's worship are continuous processes, and that any liturgy, no matter how timeless its qualities, also belongs to a particular period and culture." Cranmer, lacking our belief in progress, provided a more pessimistic spin on the idea of development in his 1549 preface: "There was never any thing by the wit of man so well devised, or so sure established, which in continuance of time hath not been corrupted." He saw his work in terms of restoration, not improvement.

Within the British Isles, the Prayer Book is primarily the property of English culture. In Wales, despite the fine early translation of the book into Welsh, much Welsh religious life later became channelled into Protestant nonconformity, which until recently was the central expression of Welsh cultural identity. In Ireland, the established Protestant Church emerged as a minority body from the political and religious confusion of the sixteenth century, and it has remained so. In Scotland, a hamfisted attempt by Charles I's government to force a version of the Prayer Book onto the Kirk in 1637 provoked violence and fury which led to the Scots waging successful war on Charles's other kingdom,

England. After this unpromising start, only a small and disestablished Scottish Episcopal Church cherished the book in later years. Yet in the untidy fashion of history, in the eighteenth century, this Scottish Church and its distinctive version of the Prayer Book had an effect on a major branch of the English Church which found itself stranded in the newly independent United States of America. The bitterness of the American War of Independence made it difficult at first for the newly created "Protestant Episcopal Church of the United States of America" to find a sensible way of relating to the Church of England, so the little disestablished sister-Church in Scotland stepped into the vacuum, consecrating the first American bishops and influencing the first American Episcopalian Prayer Book in 1789. Two thirds of those who had signed the Declaration of Independence in 1776, and two thirds of those who signed the American Constitution, were Episcopalians, whose devotional life had been formed by the 1662 Book of Common Prayer.

Alongside the British and American story is that of the second British Empire: the new ventures of British power throughout the world once the first Empire in north America had been lost. In the century after George III's loss of his thirteen American colonies, Britain reasserted itself as a world power, with a new colonial empire of extraordinary geographical extent: Africa, Asia, Australasia. The Church of England was to be found working throughout this empire, and eventually beyond it. Alongside it, the Episcopal Church of the United States also undertook missions across the globe. What started nearly half a millennium ago as Henry VIII's quarrel with the Pope in a single corner of Europe has now turned into a worldwide family of

Churches, now known by a descriptive family name hardly used before the nineteenth century: the "Anglican Communion". There is no pope or patriarch to exercise authority in this dispersed and highly diverse collection of churches: no common bond apart from the recognition of each other's clerical ministers, based on the memory of a shared history and the identity which it has created. That shared memory is symbolized especially by the practice of worship according to the tradition first created by Thomas Cranmer in the Tudor age. The Book of Common Prayer, in a flurry of different guises and versions, still gives unity to Anglicanism, one of the major elements of the Christian mosaic.

The Content of the Book

The preface of the book, explaining the motives behind its compilation, opens with a section written by the 1662 revisers. Their first thought was to hammer home an idea of Anglicanism as deliberately occupying the centre ground, a notion which has become familiar to later Anglicanism, but which would have seemed very controversial in Cranmer's revolutionary Church a century before: "It hath been the wisdom of the Church of England, ever since the first compiling of her Publick Liturgy, to keep the mean between the two extremes." This sense of being a middle way (*via media*) is one which the Anglican Communion has come to cherish, seeing itself as standing between Protestantism and Roman Catholicism—not a notion which Cranmer would have cherished! Yet there is indeed the sense of an old world shaping a new if one considers the helpful tables at the beginning of the book. The "Calendar" of the Church's year from Advent through the interminable Sundays after

Trinity is (particularly since the 1662 revision) respectably strewn with special sacred occasions: saints' days (saints from the New Testament, the early Church and the history of England), plus the ancient feasts and seasons of the Christian year, like Christmas, Lent, Easter, the Ascension of Jesus, Lammastide. While pruning what it saw as Roman excess, Anglicanism has preserved this rhythm of festival and fast where many Protestants have rejected it.

The first two series are the regular performance of prayer, praise and scripture readings for morning and evening: Mattins and Evensong. Day by day during the course of any one month, they provide for the recital of the entire 150 psalms, which are set out later in the book with useful notes to show on which day each is to be used. It is worth noticing that these psalms are still presented in the language of Miles Coverdale from the 1539 Great Bible, not in the later version of the "Authorized" or "King James" Bible of 1611. So in psalm 23, "The Lord is my shepherd: therefore can I lack nothing"—not "The Lord is my shepherd; I shall not want." As the round of the psalms is repeated, the whole of human experience of the divine unfolds: not just awe or praise, but bewilderment, anger and even downright savagery. That is why it is so important that the Psalter is recited all the way through, not making any cuts to avoid offending our modern squeamishness. Human beings are there, warts and all.

At the heart of the book is the Holy Communion service. Cranmer unsuccessfully tried to ensure that this would become the chief service of each Sunday in the parishes of England, and he would have been pleased to know this has become the norm in Anglican worship today. Preceding the service itself is the complete cycle of biblical readings at

Communion for the year, together with a short seasonal prayer for every Sunday and every major holy day. These prayers are the collects, eighty-four in all, although there are further examples elsewhere in the book. They may be considered the ultimate examples of Cranmer's genius: for the most part they translate much older Latin originals, but many are his alone, and all exhibit his skill in expressing themes, moods and profound theological ideas with an almost haiku-like brevity. They are witness to Cranmer's belief (not shared by all reformers of his age) that God may not appreciate torrents of words when approached by humanity.

The following services mark the stages of human life, from birth to death. First are the Church's liturgies of membership: Baptism, commonly conveyed in infancy in the Anglican tradition, and the one sacrament whose validity is recognized across the divides of Christendom—then Confirmation, a ceremony in which the grace of baptism is reaffirmed as a child reaches more mature years. Logically linked to this is a short course of doctrinal instruction in question-and-answer form, the Catechism: a favourite educational device in the Reformation's bitter battles of ideas. Marriage follows: a service Englished by England's first married archbishop, and the first liturgy in Christian history officially to affirm that marriage could be enjoyable for human beings—"for the mutual society, help and comfort, that the one ought to have of the other". At the heart of it are ancient words which had always been spoken in English since the early Middle Ages, for they are the words by which the couple pledge themselves to each other. These are possibly the oldest phrases regularly to be used by modern English speakers.

There follow rites for coping with sickness and death, and also a thanksgiving for women for surviving childbirth, a process more closely linked to sickness and death in Cranmer's age than in the modern west. Next a service interestingly neglected in modern Anglicanism: a service of cursing, or Commination. Let adulterers, drunkards and contract killers, not to mention he that removeth his neighbour's landmark, beware. The round of services ends more cheerfully with various services appended to the original book. The first, "Forms of Prayer to be used at Sea", reflects the emergence of England as a major naval power during the seventeenth century. The form for ordaining the three clerical orders of the Church (which is known as the Ordinal), was originally published separately in 1550. Finally, the commemorative thanksgiving for the anniversary of the reigning sovereign's accession is a reminder that the Church of England still has the monarch as its supreme governor; indeed the convention that the interior of every English parish church should display the royal arms is still widely observed.

For many years there were more state services, until Queen Victoria decided that they had had their day. They were written to commemorate major milestones in the history of the Stuart royal family: Guy Fawkes's enterprising effort to remove James I and Parliament at one fiery stroke, the beheading of Charles I after the English civil wars, and the return of his son Charles II to the thrones of Britain eleven years later. Curiously, the most momentous event in later English history never received separate commemoration: the "Glorious Revolution" of 1688, in which the nation's leaders decided that they had had enough of Catholic James II. The Church of England, like many leading politicians at the time, was never quite sure how to justify James's removal, and it seems to have decided to leave well alone, rather than cause unseemly argument in church services by creating a wholly new liturgy of thanksgiving for the *fait accompli.*

The Legacy of the Prayer Book

It was a sheer accident that a functionary of Henry VIII, chosen to be Archbishop to sort out a marital difficulty, turned out to be a gourmet of words when he was set to produce a form of worship for the kingdom. His gift was precisely appropriate. Cranmer could not write poetry—and luckily, he knew it, once sadly confessing in a letter to King Henry that he had a tin ear for verse. His insight is amply confirmed by his one venture into poetry, a translation in his Ordinal of a Latin hymn, which was so awful that it had to be replaced in 1662 by John Cosin's lovely verses "Come Holy Ghost, our souls inspire". In formal prose, however—that which was needed for the liturgy—Cranmer was a master, having an exact ear for sentences which could be repeated a hundred, a thousand times, and contain no infelicity or sudden jarring note. He was not ashamed to borrow other people's texts and then tweak them patiently until they would bear a shape capable of withstanding the remorseless repetition which liturgy demands.

Cranmer deliberately intended the language of the book to be sonorous and slightly archaic: he had no intention of letting his liturgy be sneered at for being modish or inferior to the old Latin. This archaic quality was highly significant for the future of English: it saved it from being highjacked by the pompous Latin and Greek vocabulary beloved by many of Cranmer's scholarly contemporaries. Two factors make the sixteenth century crucial for very many European languages: first the spread of printing technology, which created standardized texts in large quantities and therefore tended to standardize modes of expression, and second the scholarly movement now known as humanism, which seized European universities and enjoyed enormous intellectual prestige. Humanists were enthusiastic for the culture of ancient Greece and Rome, and excitedly imported all sorts of words from Greek and Latin in order to extend the range and flexibility of vernacular languages.

Sometimes this humanist effort was genuinely enriching. Often, however, it produced overblown, embarrassingly showy results: undiscriminating praise is often lavished on Tudor English, which in reality could be self-important and broken-backed. Cranmer, however, protected the Prayer Book from humanist excess by his consciously old-fashioned diction. A competent humanist scholar himself and a notable innovator in language when he thought it appropriate, he was nevertheless fastidious in what he took from humanist vocabulary, only occasionally striking a false note or making a verbal gamble with the future which did not pay off. So one of his collects in the Ordinal may bring pleasurable bafflement to idle perusers of the Prayer Book during service-time when it urges God to "prevent us in all our doings": "go before" is a meaning of "prevent" which has long decayed. Perhaps Cranmer edited the Ordinal in more of a hurry than usual—for another phrase in it, "the immarcessible crown of glory", needed to be calmed down in 1662 to "the never-fading crown of glory". Such examples are rare. The English language's veneer of humanist borrowings, over its matrix of Anglo-Saxon with Norman-French reinforcement, has to a great extent been fixed by Cranmer's linguistic restraint.

There is more to the Prayer Book than merely its words. It provides the English roots of a multi-faceted religious tradition, which despite its international dimension, still resonates with the images of St Augustine's cathedral at Canterbury; of country churchyards where rooks caw in the trees; of small intimate communities sheltering under northern hills; of neighbouring parish churches which (with Anglican contrariness) may treat Cranmer's liturgy either with illogically Tridentine ceremonial splendour, or with a savage austerity worthy of Geneva. Moreover, without knowledge of the Prayer Book and its thought-world, so much of English literature makes less sense. John Donne, George Herbert, Laurence Sterne, Jonathan Swift, John and Charles Wesley, Gilbert White, were parsons: so were the fathers of Jane Austen, the Brontës, Dorothy L. Sayers. T. S. Eliot came to England and adopted Anglican spirituality, finding fresh inspiration in the Book of Common Prayer. A. N. Wilson, in elegiac mood, has thus meditated on Anglican culture's central place in English identity:

> Decking the church for Christmas; arranging the flowers, and the flower rotas; laughing at the eccentricities of bishops and curates and the congregations committed to their charge: such stuff would seem to have little to do with true religion to the new noddle Born Again believer. But for centuries it formed part of the fabric of our national life.[2]

The Book of Common Prayer, pivotal to all these minor and comfortable intersections between the sacred and the everyday, was intended as an approach to the divine. Perhaps the Prayer Book text is now most often experienced in the setting of Choral Evensong in the cathedral tradition:

[2] A. N. Wilson, *The Faber Book of Church and Clergy*, 1992, p. 7.

something of an irony, because Thomas Cranmer had little affection for either cathedrals or their choirs. Cranmer's attitude is all the more unfortunate because some of the best English music of the last four hundred years has been written for the performance of Evensong. Moreover, the Prayer Book's author would also be alarmed by another facet of "Evensong spirituality": its continuing popularity in an age of agnosticism and religious doubt. Here is an unintended function for Cranmer's evening texts. For those who find the classical picture of the Christian God unbelievable or alien, this Anglican performance of patterned liturgical beauty may provide a window on seriousness. Less strident and less excluding than the Christian invitation to approach the eucharistic table, Evensong's understated presentation of the sacred may yet be the solace of those who find other, more demonstrative, expressions of Christianity beyond their powers of assent.

It is indeed worth pondering the lessons which the Prayer Book might offer to those now seeking to express Christian aspirations in liturgy. That acute observer of religious change in the modern world, Don Cupitt, expressed himself trenchantly about the liturgical books which have sought to improve on Cranmer's forms:

> *The Book of Common Prayer* (1662) gives a rather vivid impression of the cultural and political world that produced it. Its replacement, the *Alternative Service Book* (1980), floats in a social vacuum, its pages containing no reference anywhere to any of the distinctive features of modern civilization.... The book moves in a Heritage limbo, pseudo-traditional and outside real history. In relation to the lives we are actually living and what is making news at the end of the twentieth century, the ASB services are the purest fantasy.

> Morally speaking, we might just as well be spending our time in church reading *The Lord of the Rings*.[3]

Can new forms of worship speak to modern society as powerfully as the Book of Common Prayer has done for four centuries? It is a central document of a culture which has produced a treasure-house of literature. The Prayer Book is a myth, in the profoundest and truest sense of the word. It remains to be seen what, if anything, can replace it.

[3] Don Cupitt, *Radicals and the Future of the Church*, 1989, pp. 138–9.

II

The Prayer Book and Our English

ii

A speech delivered at the Presentation of the Thomas Cranmer Schools Prize, Tuesday 19 December, 1989

H.R.H. The Prince of Wales

I accepted the invitation to be Patron of the Thomas Cranmer Schools Prize simply because I mind about what may loosely be referred to as our heritage. Some may say it is an exaggerated concern and, indeed, as I have discovered only too plainly, if you actually stand up and talk about the importance of our heritage and the lessons to be learned from our forebears you are at once accused of a quaint nostalgia for a picturesque, irrelevant past. It has forced me to reflect on why there is such a fierce obsession about being "modern". The fear of being considered old-fashioned seems to be so all-powerful that the more eternal values and principles which run like a thread through the whole tapestry of human existence are abandoned under the false assumption that they restrict progress. Well, I'm *not* afraid of being considered old-fashioned, which is why I am standing here at this lectern wearing a double-breasted suit and turn-ups to my trousers, ready to declaim the fact that I believe the Prayer Book is a glorious part of every English speaker's heritage and, as such, ought to be a Grade 1 listed edifice!

Do you recall that wonderful passage of Alan Bennet in *The Old Country*?

> I imagine that when it comes to the next prayer book they won't write He, meaning Him with a capital H. God will be written in lower case to banish any lurking feeling of inferiority his worshippers might feel.

I would have liked to begin with a ringing phrase from the King James Version of the Bible:

> Hearken to my words.

But the New English Bible translates the phrase in less commanding terms:

> Give me a hearing.

It might seem more humble but it also sounds less poetic: and what we have to ask ourselves, it seems to me, is whether, by making the words less poetic, you really do make them more democratic. Isn't there something rather patronising about that whole assumption?

Possibly there *are* more people today who read less well than people in the past, although I doubt it. Most people then couldn't read at all. But supposing it were true, whoever decided that for people who aren't very good at reading the best things to read are those written by people who aren't very good at writing? Poetry is for everybody, even if it's only a few phrases. But banality is for nobody. It might be accessible for all, but so is a desert.

For the Book of Common Prayer has been a spiritual

resource of English and English-speaking people for four centuries. It is a book of prayer for the whole community, devised and composed so that it might satisfy everyone. Cranmer, like the translators of the King James Bible, looked to the past as well as the present when he set about his task at a time of reformation and change; he compiled his Prayer Book in a spirit of reconciliation. To some of his contemporaries it seemed too conservative, to others too radical, but it has survived changes in Church and State that would have destroyed a liturgy less sensitive to the profound human need for continuity and permanence. The language Cranmer employed in the Prayer Book was quite deliberately "not of an age, but for all time".

And so it has survived by passing into common speech. Words and phrases from this liturgy have become part of the heritage of the English language by continuous reiteration through centuries, in public worship and private devotion. In Church of England day schools pupils used to learn by heart the great collects from the Prayer Book, a practice much despised by educationalists today. But that learning by heart, together with regular Church services where the Prayer Book was the only rite, had a genuine influence on the minds and imaginations of ordinary men and women. Though their own speech could not command the cadences and rhythms of Cranmer's prayers, because they were familiar with them they remembered them! At home, abroad, in hospitals, on battlefields, in solitude, in society, in trouble and in prosperity, these words were remembered and gave comfort and hope in the great crises of innumerable human lives.

The Book of Common Prayer reminds us of human frailty:

among the sundry and manifold changes of the world,

and at the same time of the consolation of

the means of grace and the hope of glory.

At this point it is perhaps worth recalling what George Orwell pointed out in *Nineteen Eighty-Four*: "That the best way of getting rid of history and thought is to get rid of the language of history and ideas". So he invented "Newspeak" for his nightmare communist world. Consider the following—

> We do not presume to come to this thy table, O merciful Lord, trusting in our own righteousness, but in thy manifold and great mercies.

Compare the courtesy of Cranmer's language with the crassness of the Alternative Service Book which spends much time telling the Deity what He must already know:

> Lord Jesus Christ, only Son of the Father, Lord God, Lamb of God, you take away the sin of the world: have mercy on us; you are seated at the right hand of the Father: receive our prayer. ...

and so on.

It saddens me, as no doubt it saddens some of you, that we gather to praise Cranmer's great work at a time when it has been battered and deformed in the unlikely cause of making it easier to understand. We seem to have forgotten that for solemn occasions we need exceptional and solemn language: something which transcends our everyday speech. We commend the "beauty of holiness", yet we forget the holiness of beauty. If we encourage the use of mean, trite, ordinary language we encourage a mean, trite and ordinary view of the world we inhabit.

If English is spoken in Heaven (as the spread of English as a world language makes more likely each year) God undoubtedly employs Cranmer as his speech-writer. The angels of the lesser ministries probably use the language of the New English Bible and the Alternative Service Book for internal memos.

The editors of the Revised Standard Version and the New English Bible had good reason for many of the changes they made to the King James Version. But a good many *more* changes were made just to lower the tone, in the belief that the rest of us wouldn't get the point if the word of God was a bit over our heads. But the word of God is *supposed* to be a bit over our heads. Elevated is what God is. And for meddling with the Prayer Book there isn't even the scholarly excuse. The idea is to put great thoughts within our reach by altering the words. But the words *are* the thoughts. Admittedly the King James Version of the Bible asks us, "Why take ye thought for raiment?" But words aren't just decoration. They are the structure itself, as the Revised Standard Version inadvertently proves, by asking us: "And why are you anxious about clothing?" We can have a prayer book that talks like that if we want to—a prayer book that talks like us on a bad day. But what will it say to us on a *really* bad day? Where is the comfort in a phrase too banal to be remembered? How can we be lifted up by a sentence which itself needs lifting, on a stretcher?

"And if the salt have lost his savour," says the King James Version, "wherewith shall it be salted?" Or as the Revised Standard Version so much less memorably puts it: "If salt has lost its taste how shall its saltiness be restored?"

Is it entirely an accident that the defacing of Cranmer's Prayer Book has coincided with a calamitous decline in literacy and the quality of English? We have rejected quality in expression, just as we have rejected quality in the buildings in which we work and educate. Fortunately many more people have begun to appreciate the extent of the problem we face and have seen the fundamental need for quality, for a respect for tradition, for humility before the ideas and practices of our forebears which served them so well, and for which we have yet to find anything like an effective replacement.

It is a remarkable fact that in these islands we have produced the world's most successful language. That language has also served as the medium for some of the greatest literature in the world, including that of probably the greatest playwright who ever lived. Yet a great many people today look in dismay at what is happening to that language in the very place where it evolved. Looking at the way English is used in our popular newspapers, our radio and television programmes, even in our schools and our theatres, they wonder what it is about our country and our society that our language has become so impoverished, so sloppy and so limited—that we have arrived at such a dismal wasteland of banality, cliché and casual obscenity.

It leads me to wonder, for instance, how Hamlet would deliver his great "To be or not to be" soliloquy in the language of today—

> To be or not to be, that is the question,
> Whether 'tis nobler in the mind ...

no, we can't have all that incomprehensible, high-flown stuff. What about this?

> Well, frankly, the problem as I see it at this moment in time is whether I should just lie down under all this

> hassle and let them walk all over me, or whether I should just say "O.K., I get the message," and do myself in. I mean, let's face it, I'm in a no-win situation, and quite honestly I'm so stuffed up to here with the whole stupid mess that I can tell you I've just got a good mind to take the quick way out. That's the bottom line. The only problem is, what happens if I find that when I've bumped myself off there's some kind of a, you know, all that mystical stuff about when you die, you might find you're still—know what I mean?

In the last two decades we have witnessed a situation where our education has no longer been centred on the idea that the English language is an enormously precious legacy to be handed on. We have seen the abandonment of learning the rules of grammar and the parts of speech as boring and irrelevant. Learning poetry by heart has been abandoned, together with the idea of English as something really to be *learned*, by effort and application, by long and careful familiarity with those who had shown how to clothe their thought in the most precise, vivid and memorable language.

Of course there have been honourable exceptions to this rule where people have been courageous enough to withstand the accusations of being old-fashioned and reactionary. But the situation persists. At one of the country's leading public schools, for instance, I gather that George Eliot's *Middlemarch* was recently rejected from this year's list of "A"-level English set texts because it was thought too long and difficult.

Before I am accused of being unfair to teachers, let me hasten to add that I do not envy the task that teachers have, particularly in inner city schools. It must frequently appear a thankless task, and I know that there are many who have been trying to uphold standards amidst the general spread of mediocrity. They need our sympathy and support in an exhausting task. English teachers inevitably have to teach their pupils what is relevant, but surely they should not teach *only* what is relevant. There is also a need, through great literature, to give their pupils—in A. N. Whitehead's phrase—"the habitual vision of greatness".

We do, of course, have to recognize that we need ever higher standards if we are to survive in the modern competitive world. Our economic environment requires clarity in expression and precision in meaning. The world of work demands high standards of accuracy in communication skills to deploy and transmit facts, to process information, to persuade people, to sell goods. Many of you are familiar with computers and know that if you give these machines inaccurate instructions your wishes will not be obeyed. So it is with people. If we do not communicate effectively with one another then we create confusion and lose our way.

Inevitably there has been controversy about the standards of English teaching in schools and about children's linguistic ability. This concern is not new. Complaints that young people cannot write grammatically, spell accurately, or express themselves clearly can be found stretching back into the last century. But there is now I think a growing consensus on what needs to be taught, and it is heartening to witness the widespread recognition of this in the new national curriculum for English. It emphasizes the importance of spelling, listening, reading and writing. It recognizes the fact that competence in English is a key to success in all other subjects in the curriculum and a pre-requisite for adult life.

In the words of Saki—"You can't expect a boy to be depraved until he has been to a good school!" Today's prize is not merely an ode to antiquity. It is a demonstration of pride in our heritage. It recognizes the contribution which that heritage makes to our daily life and to assuring the achievement of standards of quality that will serve our own children well into the future. Those standards are important because they help us to enlarge our own awareness, to heighten and deepen our experience of life like nothing else can.

Dr Johnson once remarked, "I know of no good prayers but those in the Book of Common Prayer." Ours is the age of miraculous writing machines but not of miraculous writing. Our banalities are no improvement on the past; merely an insult to it and a source of confusion in the present. In the case of our cherished religious writings, we should leave well alone, especially when it is better than well: when it it great. Otherwise we leave ourselves open to the terrible accusation once levelled by that true master of the banal, Samuel Goldwyn: "You've improved it worse."

III
The Liturgy: Experiments and Results

Roger Homan

1 Provisionality

The prompting of the Liturgical Movement worldwide has been attributed to Giuseppe Sarto who became Pope Pius X in 1903; within the Anglican communion there is a case for relating the revival of the spirit of worship to the Oxford Movement,[1] though the Tractarians did not depart from the use of the Book of Common Prayer. Certainly, the unsettlement of the traditional forms dates back further than 1945 when Dom Gregory Dix, an Anglican Benedictine, published his influential book *The Shape of the Liturgy*.

1.1 Series 1

In the early 1960s the Book of Common Prayer was in general use in England's parish churches. Seldom, however, was it followed to the letter: abbreviations and variations had been practised for some years. A form that had been favoured in Anglo-Catholic churches since the 19th century was the so-called "interim rite" which involved the con-

[1] J. H. Srawley, *The Liturgical Movement: its Origin and Growth*, 1954, pp. 7–9.

junction of the Prayer of Oblation and the Lord's Prayer with the Prayer of Consecration. Again, since 1928 it had become common practice to use Jesus' summary of the Law in place of the Ten Commandments set out in the 1662 Book of Common Prayer. In a move to regularize the use of these variations, they appeared in a booklet believed to have come from the desk of the Archbishop of Canterbury Michael Ramsey. They were authorized for a period of fourteen years as "Series 1". The Series 1 Holy Communion service was a reordering of the Prayer Book form but not a rewording of it.

1.2 Series 2

In March 1965 Parliament passed the Prayer Book (Alternative and Other Services) Measure. In December of that year the Liturgical Commission published its "Draft Order for Holy Communion" in *Alternative Services Second Series*. The year 1966 was one of Convocation debates, group meetings, compromise, withdrawal of compromise and eventual publication, subject to agreement by the House of Laity in 1967. "The Church of England," wrote a member of the Liturgical Commission, "is now well on the way with the revision of the Prayer Book."[2]

What was to become known as "Series 2" took over in a big way. In form and content it was a radical departure from the Book of Common Prayer. With Series 2 Holy Communion the user-friendly booklet form came into its own, as did the sense of the ephemeral. Alternative services were presented as sequences of numbered paragraphs; Series 2 was commended as "an extremely easy system of reference". From now on the number of the paragraph, the

[2] C. O. Buchanan, *A Guide to the New Communion Service*, 1966, p. 3.

colour of the booklet and the desired posture of the congregation were to become the stuff of public announcement: the leading of worship gave way to the conduct of worshippers. To keep the people together it was deemed necessary to set out paragraph 29 (previously known as the Lord's Prayer) in lines rather than as continuous prose so that they would know when to breathe.[3]

Cranmer's Collect for Purity was retained verbatim while his Prayer of Humble Access and post-communion thanksgiving were used in an abbreviated form. The Gloria was slightly amended, the Creed retained in its 1928 version. The Sanctus remained intact. Bold sub-headings emphasised the structural division of Ante-communion (paragraphs 1–16) and Communion (paragraphs 17–20).

But even as Series 2 was being commended, there was an ominous warning from within the Liturgical Commission that the retention of elements of 1662 and 1928 would not hold. Colin Buchanan wrote:

> The conservative approach to the revision of these texts is only temporary. Moves are afoot to get an ecumenically agreed translation of each of them.[4]

The keynote of the late 1960s was menacing provisionality and this persisted in subsequent decades. The Church in its 1965 Measure authorized experiment, in practice found to be irreversible. Series 2 was offered in its day as a transient form authorized for an experimental period of three years. In the words of Ronald Jasper, Chairman of the Liturgical Commission,

> ... no attempt was made to produce a substantial work explaining its content and structure. The Liturgical

[3] *Ibid.*, p. 13.
[4] *Ibid.*, p. 12.

> Commission then felt that as this was only a "first stage" in the process of liturgical reform, a more useful purpose would be served if any explanation were reserved until later.

Its successor Series 3, however, which represented the abrupt change to modern language and was the source of "also with you", was to be more settled: "... We hope ... that Series 3 will be allowed to remain substantially as it is for some time to come."[5] But the fact was that Series 2 had become more popular than Buchanan and Jasper had bargained for. In the late 1960s the Liturgical Commission conducted its own questionnaire survey of the parishes to measure satisfaction or otherwise with the traditional language of Series 2. Had the survey demonstrated significant dissatisfaction, the Commission would have felt justified in modernizing. In the event some three quarters of respondents expressed themselves to be content but the Commission did not allow this finding to stand in its way. Some years later the American scholar Richard Fenn conducted a detailed analysis of the conduct of the official survey and discovered an alarming measure of manipulation of data.[6] The circulation of the questionnaire had already been left to the discretion of the clergy: on their advice, respondents expressing satisfaction were disregarded as old or middle-aged, naturally conservative, cranky or bad tempered. By eliminating from the sample the returns so marked, those conducting it were able to report to the Liturgical Commission that 90% of church members were calling for change.

[5] R. C. D. Jasper (ed.), *The Eucharist Today: Studies on Series 3*, 1974, p. 1.
[6] Richard K. Fenn, "The Questionnaire on Series 2", *Faith and Worship* 9, 1980, pp. 15–17.

1.3 1.3 Series 3

Series 3 arrived on the scene in 1974 and its general form and complexion were to persist in Rite A of the Alternative Service Book 1980 and in Order One of Common Worship. Its significance may be estimated at two levels. On the one hand, there is an intellectual or élite tradition in liturgical revision. Those who belong in this company are concerned with structures in worship, with kinds of symbolism that are not always evident to the people in the pew, with ecumenical alignments, with the practice of the Early Church and with eliminating the temporal features of the traditional forms. All professions, Shaw observed, are conspiracies against the laity and the Liturgical Commissioners express their professionalism by bewildering the laity with words like *anamnesis* and *anaphora* and appeals to "the meaning ... of the original Semitic language behind the Greek".[7] They who commend to the laity a modern and simple form of words tell them that the Eucharist is divided into two parts, the *missa catechumenorum* and the *missa fidelium*.[8] For many of the faithful, however, *anamnesis* was not the most striking feature of the alternative forms. For them language and content had become timeless: relevance and contemporary feeling were achieved at the cost of devotional—even mystical—focus. The significant impact of Series 3 was its modern language with its implicit redefinition of the sacred and of the relationship of the divine to the human.

The date 1662 lends its name to what Jasper calls a "family" of liturgies. By the same token Series 3 epitomizes the modern. One of the hallmarks of the Series 3 family is the stress placed upon structure, in particular upon the division

[7] Jasper, *op. cit.*, p. 3.
[8] G.J. Cuming, "Series 3 and 1662: A structural Comparison", in Jasper, *op. cit.*, p. 34.

of the early part of the service given to instruction or the Word and the Communion, when the Bread and Wine are placed on the altar. When adult baptism was the norm, catechumens would attend the Ante-communion for instruction but withdraw from the part of the service for which they were ineligible. Curiously, then, this division revives a former practice that was appropriate in conditions that no longer apply. From the time of Justin Martyr the service began with readings from the Hebrew scriptures and from the New Testament: accordingly, the new lectionary includes readings from the Jewish scriptures whereas Cranmer had confined his readings in the eucharist to the epistles and gospels. The Peace, for which Cranmer provided words without prescribing actions, is recovered from Early Church practice:[9] of course, that similar words were uttered in the days of Justin Martyr hardly licenses some of the social and intimate exchanges that nowadays break out at the prompting of "The Peace of the Lord be always with you." In all, the professed desire is to imitate the practice of the Early Church: anything from before the fifth century has been willingly embraced, its temporal properties notwithstanding; at the same time, the Prayer Book has been set aside as archaic and rooted in the seventeenth century.

In the Series 3–Rite A tradition, the faithful assemble as a body of like-minded believers ("We believe…", "This is our faith"). Because the everyday language of the bus queue was not thought to include words like "soul" or "spirit", the whole conceptual apparatus of Christians as spiritual beings was eliminated from Rite A. The ancient response to the Peace "And with thy spirit" was replaced with the vulgar

[9] *Ibid.*

"And also with you." And the prayer used in some churches before communion, "Speak the word only and my soul shall be healed" became, "Only say the word, and I shall be healed." As we shall see below, the Church, which in the year 2000 continues to play down belief in the soul, finds it to be a burgeoning faith among the young people whom it has estranged.

1.4 Series 1 & 2 Revised

The immediate progenitor of Rite B was given a name somehow not destined to find an eternal place in the hearts of the faithful or the history of liturgical change. "Series 1 & 2 Revised" fell by the wayside when the Alternative Service Book appeared in 1980.

1.5 Alternative Service Book 1980

As early as the 1965 Measure the word *alternative* was being used in official circles. It is doubtful, however, that members had in their hearts to complement the Book of Common Prayer: the language they used in their writings signified the intention of replacing it. Colin Buchanan was talking of "revision" of the Prayer Book[10] and of Series 1 as "unsatisfactory".[11] The 1980 hardback edition was a collection of revised versions of the experimental services that were thought to be most useful for the Church. In the new book Rite A was more or less the continuation of Series 3 and Rite B was the survival of Series 2. The Alternative Service Book claimed in its opening page to be a mere supplement to the timeless formulary: "The Alternative Service Book 1980, as its name implies, is intended to supplement

[10] Buchanan, *op. cit.*, p. 3.
[11] *Ibid.*, p. 9.

the Book of Common Prayer, not to supersede it." The Alternative Service Book 1980 was published with its date as part of the title "to serve as a reminder that revision and adaptation of the Church's worship are continuous processes."

The legal life of Series 1 Holy Communion expired in the same year as that in which the Alternative Service Book was introduced, although Series 1 Marriage and Funeral services continue to be authorized. At that time the General Synod declined to reauthorize it but a number of parishes continued to use it illegally and no action was brought. In 1984 the Bishop of Birmingham brought a motion to the Synod to reauthorize Series 1 Baptism and Communion: this was passed in all three houses and by a majority of 28 to 1 in the House of Bishops but overall it did not secure the required two-thirds majority. One of the pragmatic objections to the re-authorization of Series 1, voiced in 1984 by Canon Colin Buchanan, was that it was said to be virtually available in the traditional Rite B which by then had been published within the ASB.[12] The archbishop disagreed profoundly, citing Professor Owen Chadwick's words "a religious congregation which clings tenaciously to what it knows does so from no unworthy motive—the power of sacred association penetrates into a deep affection of the heart." In his address to the Synod on 29 February 1984, the archbishop observed of Series 1:

> These Services represent the way in which the Prayer Book has been used, and is still used in many of our parishes and Cathedrals. What we have in the ASB and Rite B is simply not the same.[13]

[12] J. R. Porter, "The Series 1 Issue", *Faith and Worship* 17, 1984, p. 21.
[13] Robert Runcie, "On the Re-authorization of Series 1", in David Martin and Roger Homan (eds.) "Dialogue with Tradition", *Faith and Worship* 16, 1984, p. 20.

The General Synod has declined to authorize Series 1 but the Bishops have agreed to allow its continued use, albeit in a resolution that does not name Series 1 explicitly.

2 Change and Decay

The decline in church support dates back to the years that are claimed for the beginnings of the Liturgical Movement.[14] In the first half of the nineteenth century church attendance rose from 18% to 27% and remained steady at that level until 1900, declining to 14% in 1990.[15] From the years of liturgical innovation in the 1960s until shortly after the advent of the Alternative Service Book, the Church of England was virtually reduced to half its size.[16]

In the years since Series 1 there have been several studies which—whether by intention or accident—have illuminated the relationships of liturgical revision and numerical decline. Evidence from research lends support to three propositions:

2.1 At the local level numerical decline is associated with liturgical change.

At the time of the appearance of the Alternative Service Book 1980, the Bishop of Edmonton remarked that Prayer Book churches were in decline whereas flourishing churches were using Series 3. This contentious observation prompted a survey that was conducted in the archdeaconry of Chichester. All 105 parishes were approached and 103 responded. For each parish, electoral roll statistics were

[14] Srawley, *op. cit.*, pp. 7–9.
[15] Steve Bruce, *Religion in the Modern World: Cathedrals to Cults*, Oxford, 1996, p. 29; after Robert Currie, Alan D. Gilbert and Lee Horsley, *Churches and Churchgoing: Patterns of Religious Growth in the British Isles since 1700*, Oxford, 1977.
[16] Adrian Hastings, *A History of English Christianity 1920–1985*, 1986, p. 603; Grace Davie, *Religion in Britain since 1945: Believing without Belonging*, Oxford, 1994, p. 53.

taken from the diocesan handbooks for 1975 and 1980. This provided from official sources a measure of membership growth or decline over the five-year period. The incumbent—or, if not available, churchwarden—was then telephoned and was asked the form of worship in use at the main Sunday service and whether this had changed in the preceding five years. The results of the survey speak for themselves: [17]

	Number of Parishes	**Mean change per cent**
Non-changers		
Prayer Book		
Office 19		
Communion 4	23	+3.7
Series 2	14	+19.4
Series 3	34	-3.6
Changers		
To Series 3	12	-14.9
To Series 1 & 2 Revised	15	+3.6
Others		
Series 1; Missa Normativa	5	
Total	103	

The church authorities did what they could to discredit these embarrassing findings. One or two respondents spoke to the press denying that they had taken part in the survey.

[17] Roger Homan, "Church Membership and the Liturgy", *Faith and Worship* 9, 1980, p. 22.

Seizing on the fact that some of the data had been collected from churchwardens, the Archdeacon of Chichester issued a press statement saying the survey was unreliable, irresponsible and not to be taken seriously;[18] and the Bishop of Chichester wrote in the diocesan newsletter:

> Sociological surveys need to be regarded very critically and the assumptions behind them carefully examined. The ordinary person who has not the means to do that is well advised to take them always with a pinch of salt.[19]

Perhaps he knew, as we now know from Professor Fenn's research, quite what tricks the Liturgical Commission had played with its own survey.

If in the Chichester survey change is associated with decline, continuity is associated with stability. This correlation is to be found elsewhere in the country and in other denominations. As the champions of the Liturgical Movement were quick to recognize, "of all the major denominations it is probably the Baptist that has been least affected."[20] Further, the Baptists have consistently abstained from the ecumenical relationships in the name of which much liturgical revision is prompted. Curiously, the pattern of growth enjoyed by the Baptists has also been out of line. While adult churchgoing continued to decline in the Anglican, Roman Catholic, Methodist and United Reformed churches, it rose steadily among Baptists;[21] and when the traditional denominations fell sharply, the Baptists "were able to arrest the trend."[22]

[18] Roger Homan, "Theology and Sociology: a Plea for Sociological Freedom", *Theology* 84, 1981, p. 433.
[19] [Eric Kemp], "Sociological Surveys", *Chichester Diocesan News*, November 1980, p. 2.
[20] Neville Clark, *Call to Worship*, 1960, p. 9.
[21] Peter Brierley, *Christian England: What the 1989 English Church Census Reveals*, 1991, pp. 52, 32, 38; Peter Brierley (ed.), *UK Christian Handbook: Religious Trends 1, 1998–1999*, 1997, vol. 2, pp. 8–11.
[22] Davie, *op. cit.*, p. 61.

2.2 Modern services are inherently middle-class.

This proposition is in fact more moderate and accurate than those it is designed to contradict. At the time of the publication of ASB, the Prayer Book was being written off by many clergy as élitist. Canon Michael Saward wrote that Prayer Book supporters "all seemed to live at 'The Old Manor, Gushington-in-the-Puddle'," and Canon Townshend of Norwich had them more generally dispersed "south of the Thames in the 'mink and Martini' belt".[23]

Survey evidence has been to the contrary. At that time the Gallup organization included in its omnibus poll a small number of simple but pertinent questions such as,

> Do you prefer the traditional Lord's Prayer or a modernized version?
>
> What kind of service do you prefer for a wedding—the traditional or a modern language alternative?

One of the useful features of Gallup is that it identifies respondents by demographic variables such as age, gender, region of the country and socio-economic status. This affords an insight of differences between, say, the north of England and the south or between young and old. Gallup revealed a much higher level of preference for traditional forms among the lower socio-economic groups. For example, only 66% of those in the top socio-economic group preferred the traditional wedding service whereas at the lower end the figure rose to 77%. In response to all questions, those in the south of England were rather less fond of the traditional forms than those in other parts of the country. Even in the youngest age group (16–24 years) 75% preferred the traditional Lord's Prayer and 55% wanted lessons to be read in the Authorized Version. Mr Derek Pattinson

[23] *Church Times*, 29 February 1980; *The Times*, 14 June 1980.

who was at that time chief spin-doctor for the General Synod, greeted the survey with caution and advised on a basic principle of question design: "in any form of survey the nature of the answers is so often determined by the questions."[24] It is true that quantitative data need to be read with discernment but at the end of the day one cannot be as creative with statistics as Michael Saward and Canon Townshend were being with words.[25]

The appeal of modern services to the educated middle classes and the connection that traditional forms make with the working classes are evident not only from surveys but also from observation of three tendencies.

(1) The kind of participation promoted in modern forms of worship is selective of the more literate. They isolate particular skills such as lesson reading, the conduct of responsorial psalms and the composition and leading of intercessions. The effect is not to generalize participation but to distinguish those who can from those who cannot.

(2) The "new" churches, the neo-pentecostals, the charismatics whose worship is "lively" and whose growth is without comparison in the last ten or so years, are widely observed to appeal to the youthful and educated middle class.

(3) Conversely, the least socially privileged of religious groups, for example including the black pentecostal churches in Britain, adhere to the King James version and in extemporized prayer show themselves to be fluent in its language.

[24] *Church Times*, 13 June 1980.
[25] David Martin and Peter Mullen (eds.), *No Alternative: The Prayer Book Controversy*, Oxford, 1981, pp. 186–8.

2.3 Preference for traditional forms is stronger among marginal than among nuclear members.

One of the more consistent and disturbing findings of recent research is that those who fall away from conventional religion or dwell on its boundaries are not less spiritually-minded but more so. Grace Davie[26] demonstrates a decline in membership but not in religiosity. One finds here and there testimonies of estrangement by the inwardly devout:

> The parish church is only fifty yards from here, and the service I sometimes attend is Evensong. This is partly because the ladies with hats have come and gone in the morning and an empty church welcomes my anachoretical spirit. But it is also because Cranmer's book, though banished from the morning, still presides at Evensong. Doubtless this irregularity will soon be corrected and then, I suppose, I shall only visit this twelfth-century house unofficially.[27]

Again, the cult hero of punk rock Malcolm Maclaren, recently interviewed in the religious affairs programme *Holy Smoke*, commented that he used to go to church and he found something mystical and magical there but some years ago [reckoned to be 1980] they started trying to speak the language of the street so he decided he might as well stay on the street.

The sense that the Church has misjudged the spiritual condition of those to whom it would want to appeal has been recently attested by the findings of the BBC *Soul of Britain* poll.[28] While religious allegiance is found to be at the level of 20%, some 31% identify themselves as spiritual. The belief that human beings have a soul, unfashionable though it is in the modern language services, is held by 69%; and as

[26] Davie, *op. cit.*, p. 50.
[27] Dudley Young, "Churchgoing", *PN Review* 13, 1979, p. 30.
[28] *Soul of Britain*, BBC 1, 4 June 2000 *et seq.*

only 25% believe in forms of reincarnation, we cannot write this off as a heresy imported from oriental religion. It is evident that people are seeking support for deeply spiritual feelings and do not find these in the social and secular tendencies of the worship offered by the Church of England.

One reading of the statistical tables is that the congregations that are growing fastest are those that are centred on "lively" worship. Such an interpretation should be viewed with caution. Brierley's graphs are drawn on the basis of percentage increase or decline: so the new churches appear as the fastest growing because they started relatively recently from a zero base. Moreover, worship is not the only relevant variable: many of the new churches adopt an ultra-conservative line on some moral issues such as sexuality: it could equally well be said that people are moving away from the liberal churches and seeking firm teaching and Victorian values. Such a reading accords with the findings of Kelley[29] in the United States. The institutions that are showing a rising profile (the Orthodox, the Baptists and the pentecostals) have in common a security in themselves that is not matched by those institutions that are prepared to follow a worldly lead.

Kelley contrasts the growth of the conservative churches in North America since 1960 with a simultaneous numerical decline in ten of the mainstream churches. In the United States a conservative Christian ethic is shared by churches that are lively in their worship and those that are solemn. Their appeal is explained not in terms of their worship style but in their rejection of secular values; manifesting in common a sectarian tendency, they do not so much embrace the world as move away from it.

[29] Dean M. Kelley, *Why Conservative Churches are Growing: A Study in the Sociology of Religion*, New York, 1972.

3 Cause and Effect

Are modern language services a causal factor of decline or a panic response to it?

The relationship of decline to the cycle of liturgical innovation is problematic. It could be that the Church of England is losing numbers for one or more of a number of reasons and that it would have declined even faster had it not been for the timely introduction and frequent revision of modern language services. On the other hand it is possible that in hoping to appeal to the spirit of the age, the Church is setting aside the very treasure that would appeal to its outsiders.

An extensive survey of recently trained ordinands revealed a common pattern in theological college training: candidates were so deprived of the theory and practice of the Prayer Book that they left college feeling ill-equipped to conduct traditional services. One respondent from East Anglia complained:

> There is a great deal of use of the Prayer Book (for offices and for 8.00 a.m. Holy Communion) and of Rite B in this Diocese which is my sponsoring Diocese. However, it was very difficult to persuade the powers that be at [*college*] to give very much attention to Rite B or BCP Holy Communion and I found this a drawback during my curacy.[30]

He has every reason to be concerned: the diocese from which he came and to which he was to return registered the highest rates of churchgoing in the country.[31]

We cannot here prove cause and effect. We have, however, identified certain discomforting coincidences in the

[30] Roger Homan, *To the Altar of God: Report of an Enquiry into the Preparation of Ordinands for the Conduct of Worship in the Church of England*, University of Brighton Occasional Paper, 1995, p. 23.
[31] Brierley, 1991 *op. cit.*, pp. 72–3 and map 19.

pattern of decline and have noted significant exceptions to general trends. These may throw some light on the fact that during the 1980s the Church of England lost a fifth of its membership while the number of its clergy held steady.[32] Quite what happened in 1980 to trigger such a decline is left for the reader to speculate.

[32] Brierley, 1997 *op. cit.*, vol. 2, p. 9.

IV
Planning for Change: Suggestions and Ideas

written and produced by the Education and Communication Sub Group of the Liturgical Publishing Group

Contents

Part 1

Part 2

Part I
¶ *Understanding* Common Worship

What is *Common Worship*?

Common Worship is a series of new services which are replacing those in *The Alternative Service Book 1980* (ASB) from 1 January 2001.

The Book of Common Prayer (BCP, sometimes known as '1662' or the 'Prayer Book') is authorized permanently, but the ASB was only authorized for a limited period (originally ten years, later extended to the end of the year 2000). The process of review and revision of the ASB began several years ago. *Common Worship* is the result.

Why do we need new services?

Our world is constantly changing and our understanding of God is always developing. God may not change, but in every generation we find new ways of expressing ourselves to one another and to God. When the Church of England's only forms of service were those in *The Book of Common Prayer*, worship was theoretically fixed for hundreds of years. Yet people found other ways of adding variety and expressing themselves in new ways:

¶ They added hymns and songs;

¶ They added extra ceremony and actions;

¶ They added extra services, such as Christmas carol services and Harvest Festival.

In this century there has been a great deal of thinking about, and experimentation with, new services. This culminated in the services in *The Alternative Service Book 1980*.

ASB – 'Best Before End 2000'

When the ASB was published, no one knew which (if any) of the new services would stand the test of time. The ASB soon became an established part of the worship of the Church of England, alongside *The Book of Common Prayer*. However, after 20 years of use, the weaknesses as well as the strengths of the ASB have become apparent. The General Synod therefore decided that there was a need to revise the ASB, so that the Church could continue to draw on both modern and traditional services.

There are some specific reasons for change:

¶ There has been fresh thinking about worship, especially about the Christian year, about the use of the Bible in worship and about baptism and Christian nurture.

¶ There has been much discussion about the place of 'common prayer' (that is, shared forms of worship) in the Church of England. The result is services which have a strong and recognizable structure, but allow for variety and local choice in the content of some parts. This enables the Church to express its unity through its worship whilst allowing the mission context of the local church to determine some of the detail.

¶ A great deal of supplementary material has been produced since the ASB (such as Holy Week and Easter services and material for All Age services). It's time to consolidate all of that experience.

¶ Other denominations use many of the same words and prayers as we do and, where possible, these common forms are being revised by the different Churches in line with each other.

¶ Some parts of the ASB have proved to be weaker than others. For instance, the Funeral Service is rarely used as it is printed in the ASB. Most clergy and Readers use and adapt it to the particular circumstances of the funeral in question. New services can build in that sort of flexibility.

¶ There is a need to build connections between the Church's public worship and its pastoral ministry, so that our prayers can match our lives and our lives may be formed by what we pray. The new services provide more links between public worship and pastoral care.

¶ There has been some criticism of the language of the ASB. Some have felt that it is rather 'flat' and unpoetic in places. In addition, some parts need to be changed to make it absolutely clear that both men *and* women are being referred to, for example in lines such as, 'We have sinned against you and against our *fellow men*' (from the confession in ASB Holy Communion Rite A).

What about *The Book of Common Prayer*?

The Book of Common Prayer is authorized permanently and is completely untouched by this revision process.

From 1 January 2001 the Church of England will have two sources for its worship: *The Book of Common Prayer* and the new services, known collectively as *Common Worship*.

What's in *Common Worship*?

Common Worship consists of a main service book containing the most frequently used services, supported by other books containing material for particular needs (such as funerals and marriage). The full title of the new services, *Common Worship: Services and Prayers for the Church of England*, tells us a lot:

¶ First, it is not only a book. It is a collection of services and resources which will be published in books, as separate booklets, on simple cards, on computer disk and on the Internet.

¶ Secondly, it emphasizes the important part that worship plays in expressing our unity. It is something we have 'in common'. The Church of England tries to balance local responsibility for worship with a sense of belonging to the wider Church.

¶ Thirdly, these are services for the Church of England. We don't presume to think that our decisions will be right for every other Church, but they are designed to be usable across the whole breadth of the Church of England.

What will be in the main service book?

The main *Common Worship* service book will contain the following:

The Declaration of Assent

The Calendar

A Service of the Word
Morning and Evening Prayer on Sunday
Morning and Evening Prayer from *The Book of Common Prayer*
Night Prayer (Compline)
Night Prayer (Compline) in Traditional Language
Prayers for Various Occasions
The Litany
The Litany from *The Book of Common Prayer*
Authorized Forms of Confession and Absolution
Creeds and Authorized Affirmations of Faith

Holy Communion
- A Form of Preparation
- Order One [*the successor to Rite A*]
- Order One in Traditional Language
- Order Two [*the Prayer Book service as commonly used*]
- Order Two in Contemporary Language
- Supplementary Texts

Thanksgiving for the Gift of a Child
Holy Baptism

Collects and Post Communions
Collects and Post Communions in Traditional Language

Rules

Lectionary [*references only*]

The Psalter
Canticles

Table of Collects and Post Communions from *The Book of Common Prayer*

Index of Biblical References
General Index

The book deliberately includes both modern and traditional language and modern and traditional orders of service. The intention is to give a clear signal that both have an appropriate place in the worship of the Church of England today. The hope is that this may help to put an end to destructive and draining battles over modern and traditional forms of worship, by making the traditional more accessible to a new generation and presenting the modern as a legitimate part of the Church of England's inheritance.

Other key services

The Marriage, Funeral and Wholeness and Healing services will also be published in November, in a separate book of Pastoral Services. Within the next few years further services will be published, such as services for daily prayer during the week.

Will there be other editions?

As well as the main books, there will also be a number of services published as booklets and cards. These include Holy Communion, Baptism, Marriage and Funerals.

To make it easier for churches to produce local orders of service, all the services will also be produced on computer disks and available on the Internet (see below for more details).

There will also be a large format President's edition, a large print desk edition, and a large print edition of Order One Holy Communion. Services will also be available in Braille in due course.

What are the new services like?

Some of the new services (such as baptism) contain new material reflecting fresh thinking. Others (such as Holy Communion) are gentle revisions of the ASB. They all provide strong and recognizable structures, whilst allowing for flexibility in local use. Much of the new material will feel familiar because it draws on words from the ASB and *The Book of Common Prayer*.

The other key factor about the new services is that, unlike the ASB, they have no 'sell by' date. In the future, when a service needs changing it can be revised as and when required, while the rest remain unchanged.

How will *Common Worship* affect us?

That depends on what sort of services you now have in your church. You may have noticed some changes already. For instance, you may be using the new *Common Worship* lectionary as the basis for Bible readings, and the new baptism service is also in widespread use. Most of the remaining services will be published in the autumn of 2000.

If your church uses only services from *The Book of Common Prayer* then *Common Worship* will not necessarily affect you at all, as the BCP services remain completely unchanged. However, you might choose to use the *Common Worship* main service book for your Prayer Book-based services.

If you have services which are currently taken from the ASB, then you will notice some changes. Remember that your church may be using ASB-based services, but in locally produced booklets or cards rather than the book itself.

Who has produced *Common Worship*?

The production of a new service begins with the Liturgical Commission being asked by the General Synod or the House of Bishops to write something.

The process of producing *Common Worship* involved all parts of the Church, starting with

¶ **The Liturgical Commission**, which produced first drafts. These went to …

¶ **The House of Bishops,** which amended the material if it felt it was necessary and then sent it to …

¶ **The General Synod,** where representatives of the clergy and laity, with the bishops, debated the drafts.

¶ The drafts were also considered in **revision committees,** where further changes were made in response to the debates in Synod and suggestions sent in by Synod members and **members of the public**.

¶ When revision was complete the services were again considered by the **House of Bishops**.

¶ Finally **The General Synod** voted on the final form of the services. A two-thirds majority was required in all three houses (bishops, clergy and laity).

¶ Authorization dates were set and the process of **publication** began.

Field-testing

In addition, over 800 churches around the country tested out the first drafts of some of the new services. (Not all of the *Common Worship* services were tested in this way – some of the first services to be worked on were produced before the procedure for experimental use came into operation.)

Can we continue using our existing services?

You can carry on using any services from *The Book of Common Prayer*. Services from the ASB will no longer be authorized after 31 December 2000, being superseded by the *Common Worship* services. However, many familiar parts of the ASB services are retained in the new services and may continue to be used as part of *Common Worship*.

Some may face difficulties in completing the changeover by the end of the year. For instance, if the benefice is vacant a parish may wish to delay decisions about worship until the new incumbent arrives. For this reason the canons (rules) of the Church have recently been changed. They now allow a church to seek special permission from the bishop to continue using a particular ASB service for an initial period of up to three years. After that, permission can be sought for a further period of up to two years. Specific reasons will need to be given as to why the parish is unable to complete the changeover in time. The House of Bishops recommends that this new provision should be used 'to provide a parish with the time and space it needs to make or complete the process of introduction of the new forms of service, and not as an opportunity simply to delay that process'. Bishops *cannot* give a blanket permission to continue using the ASB services.

Part 2
¶ *Changing over to* Common Worship

What happens next?

The words on the page are just part of the picture. What matters most is the next step: churches using *Common Worship* in ways that fit the local situation, turning words into living worship. There will be decisions to be taken and maybe some fresh ideas about worship in your church will result. The aim of it all is to glorify God and to connect our worship with the worship of every time and every place – and with the never-ending worship in heaven.

When will it all be ready?

Some of it already is, and has been available for some time. Most of the rest should be published in the autumn of 2000. Some further material will appear over the next few years. Most of the services will be authorized from Advent Sunday (3 December 2000) and published in November 2000.
Here is the current situation:

Already published

¶ *Common Worship: Calendar, Lectionary and Collects.*

¶ *Common Worship: Initiation Services* (Baptism, Confirmation, Affirmation of Baptismal Faith and Reception into the Communion of the Church of England).

Being pepared for publication in November 2000

¶ *Common Worship: Services and Prayers for the Church of England* (the main service book). For details of the content, see Part 1 above.

¶ *Common Worship: Pastoral Services* (containing Marriage, Funerals, Thanksgiving for the Gift of a Child, and Wholeness and Healing).

¶ *Common Worship: Weekday Lectionary* (to complement the three-year Sunday lectionary already published). This will initially be available only in the form of an annual 'almanac'.

Material to be published within the next few years

¶ *Patterns for Worship* (provisional publication date of 2001)

¶ Ordination Services.

¶ Daily Prayer.

¶ Seasonal Material.

Where will we be able to get the *Common Worship* services?

All of the *Common Worship* services, in both printed and electronic formats, are, or will be, available through good bookshops or direct from Church House Publishing through Church House Bookshop (details below).

They will be available on disk in two forms:

¶ Plain text disks, in a popular word processing format and in 'rich text format' (which is readable by most word processing software);

¶ Modules for *Visual Liturgy*, the service planning software from Church House Publishing.

In addition, all the *Common Worship* services will be published and available free of charge on the Church of England's web site (www.cofe.anglican.org/commonworship).

All clergy have been sent a copy of the Holy Communion services to aid planning and decision-making in preparation for the authorization of the services on Advent Sunday.

Other services are available in their Synod document format from:
Church House Bookshop
31 Great Smith Street
London SW1P 3BN
Phone 020 7898 1300
Fax 020 7898 1305
Email bookshop@c-of-e.org.uk
Web www.chbookshop.co.uk

Will there be musical settings for the new services?

The Royal School of Church Music (RSCM), as the Church of England's official music agency, is coordinating the work of providing a wide range of settings for the new services in many different musical styles.

It is hoped that music for key services (such as Holy Communion) will be ready at the same time as the publication of the main *Common Worship* service book in the autumn of 2000. Some music will be provided in the President's Edition of the main service book, and other material will be available in supplementary resource books. Further settings are likely to be produced in the years to come.

Some parishes may wish to adapt settings that they already use.

How much will it all cost?

That depends on the format in which you choose to use the new services – books, booklets, service cards or locally produced orders of service. We want to make sure that *Common Worship* in all its forms is both durable and of high quality, but the prices are being kept as low as possible to make sure that the material is available to everyone.

Single copies of the main book will cost £15. However, Church House Publishing will run a special offer during June and July 2000 offering copies for £10. To qualify for the special price, orders have to be made in multiples of 20. Cheques and credit cards will be cashed and debited from 1 August. Your local bookshop may offer a discount for bulk purchases after publication, but this will almost certainly not be so great. Cards and booklets will cost from 70p to £2.95, depending on their format.

Some churches will choose to produce their own orders of service using the *Common Worship* material and use these alongside copies of the main book. Others will buy the booklets or cards for the services they use.

If you are planning to produce your own orders of service you might want to buy the relevant services on computer disk (approximately £20.00) or to buy the service-planning software *Visual Liturgy*. A new version will cost £100.00.

All the new services will also be available for FREE download from the Internet via the Church of England's web site when they are authorized for use.

For more information on the various editions, prices and discounts see the marketing materials from Church House Publishing which will be sent out after Easter.

For advice and guidance on producing local orders of service see *Producing Your Own Orders of Service* by Mark Earey (CHP / *Praxis*, £7.95).

How can we get the information we need?

Marketing materials from Church House Publishing will keep clergy and others aware of what is being published.

The church press (*Church Times, Church of England Newspaper*, etc.) will carry reports on the *Common Worship* services. In the meantime there are three other easy ways to keep up to date:

¶ The latest news on the new services is available on the Church of England's web site (www.cofe.anglican.org/commonworship). You will find the text of this booklet and other resources there as well.

¶ *News of Liturgy* costs 50p each month and is available from Grove Books Ltd., Ridley Hall Road, Cambridge CB3 9HU, Telephone 01223 464748, Fax 01223 464849.

¶ *Praxis News* is produced quarterly by *Praxis*, an education and training agency supported by the Liturgical Commission. It includes the latest news of the new services, presented in a way to make it easier for you to share with others in your church. Its content is also available via the Internet for adapting and pasting into your parish magazine or notice sheet. *Praxis News* costs £4 per year and is available from *Praxis* Resources, Sarum College, 19 The Close, Salisbury SP1 2EE

Phone 01722 424827
Fax 01722 338508
Email praxis@sarum.ac.uk
Web www.sarum.ac.uk/praxis/

Praxis also produces training resources to assist those explaining the new services to others (such as those introducing the services to a PCC or congregation). For more information, contact *Praxis* Resources at the Sarum College address above.

Who can make the decisions?

Most decisions about forms of service used in a parish are taken by the incumbent and the Parochial Church Council (or equivalent). Some churches have a worship committee or worship leaders' meeting (which may or may not be a sub-committee of the PCC). Such a committee may well make a recommendation to the PCC.

The final decision about forms of service for Sunday or other regular worship rests with the incumbent and PCC together. In moving from ASB to *Common Worship*, PCCs and clergy will need to discuss the options and forms of service available and decide which *Common Worship* services will best meet their current needs. In some circumstances a church will want to keep a sense of continuity with ASB services, and the choice will be obvious. In other churches the decision-making may provide the opportunity for a change in the form of service. Either way, the whole PCC will need to make and record a clear decision.

For services such as marriages and funerals decisions about the form of service are taken by the minister responsible for the service, normally working in consultation with the family or individuals concerned.

How can we introduce the new services?

To make the most of the new services each church will need to have planned the way they will be introduced. Further resources to help with introducing the new services will be sent to all churches in September.

Grasping a golden opportunity

If we are to make the most of the new material, we need to see it as an opportunity to renew our whole understanding of public worship and of the individual services in question.

Getting down to details

Each parish needs to have a strategy for imparting information, facilitating discussion and deepening understanding. Here are some suggestions for action:

¶ Put it on the PCC agenda urgently.

¶ Use items from *Praxis News*, *News of Liturgy*, the Church of England's web site, or this booklet in your parish magazine. Simply cut and paste, or put things in your own words.

¶ Distribute copies of this booklet, or the accompanying leaflet to your whole congregation. Further copies may be ordered from Church House Publishing at the address given below.

¶ Each diocesan bishop has been asked to designate someone to oversee the changeover to *Common Worship* – make contact with the relevant person in your diocese.

¶ Find out what training events are being put on by your Diocesan Liturgical Committee (or equivalent), diocesan training team or *Praxis*. Take a group from your parish to those that are near you.

¶ Are you planning a parish weekend away? Why not make worship and liturgical change a major matter for discussion?

¶ Consider using existing small groups (such as home groups, youth groups, Mothers' Union, etc.) as places where these matters can be aired. Further background materials will be sent to all clergy in September to help with this.

¶ Why not plan to run a special Advent course of church meetings or small groups to share what is happening? Or plan now to make worship part of your study in Lent 2001, with a thorough look at the theology and history of Christian worship and how the new services fit into these.

Finding useful material

A range of publications which will help in the understanding and the use of the new services will accompany the publication of *Common Worship*. Here is a selection:

¶ *Using Common Worship* – a series of short books on the main *Common Worship* services, including Holy Communion, Funerals, Marriage and Initiation – explaining the thinking behind the services and full of practical ideas for using them. Produced by CHP in partnership with *Praxis*, they will be published in the autumn.

¶ *Understanding Worship: A Parish Study Guide*, produced by *Praxis*, to be published by Continuum in February 2001.

¶ *Common Worship Today*, a revision of *Anglican Worship Today*, produced by the Group for the Renewal of Worship (GROW), to be published by HarperCollins in November 2000.

¶ Paul Bradshaw (ed.), A *Companion to Common Worship*, produced by The Alcuin Club, to be published by SPCK in 2001.

¶ Michael Perham, *A New Handbook of Pastoral Liturgy*, to be published by SPCK in 2000.

¶ Relevant booklets in the Grove Worship Series – details from
Grove Books Ltd.
Ridley Hall Road
Cambridge
CB3 9HU
Phone 01223 464748
Fax 01223 464849

What decisions do we need to take?

Each church or other worshipping community will have different needs and different resources. The following table is intended as a guide for PCC decision-making:

Question	Considerations	Possible Action
Do you need to use Common Worship services at all?	Unless your church wishes only to use BCP services from existing Prayer Books, you will need *Common Worship*.	**Get hold of copies of the relevant new services (see above).**
Do you need to apply for special permission to use ASB services beyond 2000?	Bishops can give time-limited permission to continue using ASB services, but only where there is good reason to delay the changeover to *Common Worship*. They cannot give blanket permission to carry on with the ASB indefinitely.	**Consider your reasons (if any) for delaying.** **Apply to the bishop if appropriate.**
Which Common Worship Services will be used?	Any services which are currently taken from, or based on, the ASB will require *Common Worship* material. The main *Common Worship* service book includes both modern services and services in traditional language based on the BCP as 'commonly used'. Many churches have a mix of Prayer Book and modern services. It may be that the new book will be useful for both sorts of service in your church, or you may wish to continue using your existing BCP for services from *The Book of Common Prayer*. Take particular care over decisions about Holy Communion services. *Common Worship* has four orders from which to choose. Don't forget to consider what you will need for funerals and marriage services.	**Make a list of the services which will need *Common Worship* material. Identify which form of service will be used for each.**
What formats of Common Worship services will be most appropriate in your church (i.e. books, booklets, cards, something produced locally)?	Depending on how many services you intend to have which are based on *Common Worship*, and the size of your congregations, you will need to decide: ¶ Whether to buy copies of the main service book (and how many); ¶ Whether to use the published booklets (and how many you will need and for which services); ¶ Whether to use the published service cards (and how many you will need and for which services); ¶ Whether to produce your own orders of service for some or all of the services you need; ¶ Whether to use some combination of the above (e.g. books for some services, your own leaflet for others).	**Check on the prices for the published books, booklets and cards (including bulk discounts).** **Explore the cost and practicalities of producing your own orders of service for some services. The book *Producing Your Own Orders of Service* (CHP/*Praxis*, £7.95) contains much more information that will help you in your decision-making.**

	Maybe you don't feel ready to make these decisions yet. You could produce an inexpensive local order of service ready for the changeover deadline (1 January 2001) and make decisions about purchasing materials, after you have used the services for a while. You will miss out on the full pre-publication discount, but bulk discounts may still be available if you shop around although these are likely to be lower than the May/June offer.	
Do you need to raise some money in order to pay for the decisions taken above?	There are budget implications for all of the options above. Books and booklets bought off the shelf have initial costs, but will usually last several years. Home-produced orders of service tend not to last as long, and may need initial investment in hardware or software, and regular replacement. It is tempting to consider a scheme such as inviting congregation members to pay for a copy of the main book (perhaps in memory of a loved one) – but beware of sowing the seeds of a future problem (see below). Some congregation members will want to buy a personal copy of the book to have at home. By encouraging them to buy through your church you may be able to order more copies and take advantage of bulk discounts.	**Decide on a scheme to pay for whatever book booklets, cards or locally-produced order of service you will need.** **Make sure the congregation is aware of what is going on; encourage those who want to buy a copy of the *Common Worship* main book for personal use at home to do so through the church.**
Consider what to do with old ASBs (if you have copies).	Some ASBs (and ASB booklets) are in poor condition and may best be disposed of via your local paper-recycling centre. In some churches ASBs were given in memory of loved ones or by members of the congregation. There may be a pastoral need to treat these more carefully. For instance, donors of ASBs might be invited to take copies home. Where donors are no longer traceable, congregation members could be offered the chance to take them. You could consider establishing a book of remembrance in which to record the names of those in whose memory ASBs were given, or even preserve the presentation plates from ASBs.	**Consider what books and booklets you have that are no longer needed.** **If appropriate, check out the practicalities of paper recycling.**
Consider how to move on from the ASB.	For many in the Church of England today the ASB is symbolic of an important and positive era of worship in the church and in their own Christian lives. In changing over to *Common Worship* it will be important to affirm all that was good about the ASB and its services. It may be appropriate to include such sentiments in any service to inaugurate the use of the new services. (More material to help with this will be forthcoming in September.)	**Find ways of allowing people to express feelings of gratitude for the ASB and sadness (or fear, or whatever) at its passing – for instance, there may be ways of using the church magazine for this.**

Consider when to begin using the new services.	The new lectionary and initiation services are already available and authorized and may be used immediately (if you are not using them already). Most of the other services will be authorized from Advent Sunday 2000. The ASB services may be used until 31 December 2000 (unless you have received permission from your bishop to continue using them beyond December 2000). ¶ You might decide to begin using new services from Advent Sunday. ¶ You might decide to begin using new services from 1 January 2001.	**Make sure you have ordered or planned to buy any books, booklets or cards you need ahead of your planned start date.** **If you are planning to produce your own orders of service, make sure they will be ready by your chosen start date.**
Consider the implications for others.	Other people may be affected by any decisions you take and will need to be kept informed: ¶ Musicians: choir, organist, music group, etc.; ¶ Children and young people and the leaders of their groups; ¶ Local schools with which you have contacts, especially church schools; ¶ Those involved in ministries such as baptism preparation, post-funeral bereavement visiting, marriage preparation, and so on.	**Identify those affected and plan how and when to communicate the changes to them, and who will do it.** **Make plans for any fresh training needed for these people.**

This booklet was written and produced by the Education and Communication Sub Group of the Liturgical Publishing Group.

For additional copies please contact Church House Publishing on telephone 020 7898 1451 or at the address below.

For further information about any of the matters covered in the booklet and the *Common Worship* process in general, please contact
Dr Colin Podmore
Secretary to the Liturgical Publishing Group
Central Secretariat
Telephone 020 7898 1385
Fax 020 7898 1369
at the address below.

Church House
Great Smith Street
London
SW1P 3NZ

Email common.worship@c-of-e.org.uk
Web www.cofe.anglican.org/commonworship

V

Common Prayer and the Pirates

A modified and expanded version of a paper delivered to and published by the Manchester branch of the Prayer Book Society, November 1997

A. C. Capey

I first touched on this matter in 1991. I had been asked to put down my thoughts on the kind of points the Prayer Book Society might usefully make in its invited submission to the Liturgical Commission. What became of my paper, which was very different in both tone and detail from the document eventually submitted, I do not know; but I did print a little bit of it in *Faith and Worship*, the bit that concerned what I had come to regard as an act of piracy by the Commission on the province of Common Prayer. I could point to the grounds for my suspicion, but it was at that stage only a suspicion. After all, barely ten years earlier the Alternative Service Book 1980 had been carried triumphally on a cushion into Westminster Abbey (I see still in my mind's eye the smirks of assurance on the processing synodsmen), and the assumption that our Common Prayer would quietly fade away, displaced by the vibrant and mould-breaking ASB, was assiduously peddled by forward-looking bishops and archdeacons: "You're not still using *this*, surely?" a visiting dignitary asked of the Rector of Mobberley. "It's time to bring the parish on!" As recently as 1988, that was still the approved approach, the official line. "If we do not dwell on the Prayer Book's strength today," declared the Lambeth Conference bishops, "it is because we judge its era is slipping irretrievably into the past. The book's language is that of another age."—Yes: so is Shakespeare's, Milton's, Bunyan's: the point is not that such language is "time-honoured" (a familiar adjective of condescension in the "generous" idiom of the other side) but that it is indefinitely re-readable, rewarding the re-reading, as the present generation, given the chance, will testify.

You can read the late David Scott's anatomization of those bishops' views in *Faith and Heritage*, No. 27. It is not now my purpose to enjoy a "slaughterous field-day" at the expense of misguided bishops. My purpose here is to track the change of direction in the Liturgical Commission since 1989–90, a change involving its adoption of the notion of Common Prayer, and to question whether the Prayer Book Society should co-operate with the Commission in what has effectually become an invasion of the very territory that the Lambeth bishops treated in so supercilious and dismissive a manner not two years before.

Common Prayer belongs to the nation; it was created for us out of, and taking theological exception to, various departmental service-books and other documents; it was recovered for us, in defiance of the Presbyterian Directory, in 1662; it was retained for us, in defiance of William III's desired "comprehension" (a sort of home-centres ecumenical venture, commended for its "flexibility" by Dr Jasper[1]); it comfortably resisted Unitarian depredations in the 18th century; it was the linch-pin of the Tractarian movement; it was only cautiously modified in 1928, in an attempt to keep the Anglo-Catholics away from the lure of the English Missal. The book belongs to us all, even if only a tiny proportion of the tiny proportion that attends church today actually prays it; certainly it isn't the peculiar property of the even tinier element in the nation that subscribes to the Prayer Book Society.—So: What can be the objection to the Liturgical Commission's apparent attempt to recall the church to Common Prayer? Is not the change of wind in the Commission to be welcomed by the Prayer Book Society?

When its *Patterns for Worship* appeared in 1989, the Liturgical Commission hadn't quite decided upon, or was not ready to divulge, its ultimate objective. Common Prayer—the notion of it, and the practice—was then mocked as an unreal fiction.

> "Common prayer" does not in fact exist, in the sense of being able to walk into any church in the land and find exactly the same words to follow. Nor should we pretend that it would be either good or right to return to a position—well over a century ago—when that might have been the case.[2]

Instead, an alternative meaning of *common* was suggested:

> Rather, "common prayer" exists in the Church of England in the sense of recognizing, as one does when visiting other members of the same family, some com-

[1] See "Escape from Schism", pages from Macaulay's *History* edited by J. Enoch Powell (*Faith and Worship* 24), and *Faith and Worship* 30, in which R. C. D. Jasper's book *The Development of Anglican Liturgy* (1989) was reviewed under the title "A Whig's Interpretation of History".

[2] P. 5; text of first sentence *sic*: does common grammar still exist?

> mon features, some shared experiences, language and patterns or traditions.[3]

The question is raised, "Do these proposals undermine Common Prayer in the Church of England?"[4] and under that heading the Commissioners "identify three aspects of the Anglican understanding of common prayer" which do not include the common understanding of the phrase to mean the Book of Common Prayer.

So the Common Prayer Book was deemed to exist today as only one of several "resources" of common worship: Dr Jasper's "flexibility" and "variety" were the key words.

> To accept a variety of forms, dictated by local culture, is part of our Anglican heritage, spelt out by Archbishop Thomas Cranmer in his 1549 Preface: "it often chanceth diversely in divers countries."[5]

In laying claim to Cranmer's authority for its offered "variety of forms" the Commission, however, overreaches itself. Cranmer wrote, in a text available in every copy of the Book of Common Prayer,

> And whereas heretofore there hath been great diversity in saying and singing in Churches within this Realm, some following *Salisbury* use, some *Hereford* use, and some the use of *Bangor,* some of *York,* some of *Lincoln,* now from henceforth all the whole Realm shall have but one use.[6]

Cranmer, that is, was proudly announcing the exact opposite of what the Liturgical Commission reports him as "spelling out". The invocation of "our heritage" at this

[3] *Ibid.*
[4] P. 288.
[5] *Ibid.*
[6] Preface to the 1549 *Booke of the Common Prayer* reprinted in our Prayer Book as "Concerning the Service of the Church".

moment is undercut by the Commissioners' apparent unacquaintance with this very well-known part of our heritage. Cranmer's book was to be not Salisbury Use, not York, not Hereford, but one book for *all* the English: hence Common Prayer. The Commissioners' quotation is in fact not, as they state, from the 1549 Preface but from an appendix, also reprinted in every copy of the 1662 Book under its original title "Of Ceremonies". Here, as well as saying a thing that must stick in the gullet of many a reformer, that "they cannot reasonably reprove the old only for their age", Cranmer ends up by asserting that the intention is not to "prescribe any thing but to our own people only":

> For we think it convenient that every country should use such Ceremonies as they shall think best to the setting forth of God's honour and glory, and to the reducing of the people to a most perfect and godly living, without error or superstition; and that they should put away other things, which from time to time they perceive to be most abused, as in men's ordinances it often chanceth diversely in divers countries.

The English Reformers had no imperialistic ambitions to impose their ceremonies on Wittenberg or Geneva or even Rome, and the language of Common Prayer need not be English even in England: as declared in the 1549 Preface, "Yet is it not meant, but that when men say Morning and Evening Prayer privately, they may say the same in any language that they themselves do understand." French, also, was used at Calais. But the determination to have one form of prayer for England was absolutely plain both in 1549 and 1552. The practice of including a copy of the Act for the Uniformity of Common Prayer began in some 1552 editions. Cranmer was not speaking of "variety of forms" such as we now have, or of submitting to the dictates of "local culture", but of each national church's need to "put away... things, which from time to time [are perceived] to be most abused," which abuses take different forms in different countries. The notion of common prayer in the Book of Common Prayer is plain and clear: the Book does demand uniformity. The reader's trust in the writer has been betrayed. (Nothing new in that, you may say: the Preface to the ASB disguises the true reading of the Royal Commission's report in 1906.) Let us not guess whether this was a sign of the Commission's difficulties with reading or a blandly dishonest impertinence; whether done through ignorance, or through their own deliberate fault. Neither alternative inspires confidence. Both serve equally well the hidden agenda of claiming for English tradition a sense of the word *common* which it has never had in the Church of England.

Behind the spurious claim to be fulfilling Master Cranmer's will, however, may be observed the earliest change of tack from the Lambeth bishops' judgement. Perhaps the Commission had begun to suspect that the Prayer Book would not, after all, simply slip irretrievably into the past. Certainly, by 1991, the Commission has clearly shifted its position. In its report *The Worship of the Church*[7] the key word is no longer "flexibility" or "variety" but "unitive". Conscious of the "divisive" effect of the Alternative Service Book 1980 *vis-à-vis* the Book of Common Prayer, and wishing "to draw [the traditions (*sic*)] closer together"[8], the Commission aims to encourage in the

[7] GS Misc 364, para. 23, p. 10.
[8] Para. 6, p. 5.

rest of us the "degree of convergence" that its members have already attained by "eating and worshipping together".[9] "The Church [has] been working for too long with ... too wide [a] range of alternatives." What is needed is "a unitive doctrinal sensitivity" and "a sense of Common Prayer"—which would include "the continuing existence and use of the BCP".

On the face of it, that's a substantial concession to the Prayer Book Society—and indeed it coincides with the Commission's approach to the society for "talks" and precedes by not many months a conference in which P. D. James and David Martin spoke for the Prayer Book Society and when lip-service (at least) was paid to the Book of Common Prayer as the "model and inspiration" of all new services.[10]

We should be wary, however, of Greeks bearing gifts. The "common heritage" that we were invited to "explore together" includes *Patterns for Worship*, in which there is set down the bald recommendation to "Address God as you" and the opinion that though "Cranmer recognised that people need time and repetition to make the liturgy their own, we need to do it without a string of dependent clauses." "Cranmer's relative pronoun"[11], the beginning of his strings of dependent clauses, ordinarily requires thee/thou/thy, the pronoun on which the Liturgical Commission had, as a matter of principle, pronounced anathema; there was to be no negotiation over that—if we would go forward, we must renounce the 2nd person singular.

[9] Para. 9, p. 6.
[10] *Model and Inspiration: The Prayer Book Tradition Today*, ed. Michael Perham, 1993. It should in fairness be said that the published texts show very little common ground between Colin James and David Stancliffe on the one hand, P. D. James and David Martin on the other.
[11] The phrase is the title of an article by J. Enoch Powell, *Faith and Worship* 26.

Moreover, in *The Worship of the Church* Common Prayer is habitually distinguished from the Book of Common Prayer. The Commission aims to promote the "sense of Common Prayer" without the book (which would be allowed to continue to exist... [How kind! As if any ASB ordination could proceed without explicit acknowledgment of the fundamental authority of the Book of Common Prayer, the Ordinal and the Articles!]) But would the notion have come into being without the creation and maintenance of the book, which used to be called just Common Prayer? The title *The Booke of the Common Prayer* goes back to 1549, and for example The Revd Thomas Aylesbury, in 1656, had the book not the notion in mind when he wrote: "Is not thy vineyard laid waste, thy breasts dried up, thy Common Prayer and administration of the Sacraments laid aside, and the glory of thy Liturgy departed?"[12] Does not the notion derive from the book, take its meaning from the book? The pirate-Commissioners cannot stomach that argument, hence their hatching of a sentence that appears to give ground ("generously") while in fact conceding nothing:

> ...while recognizing that the B[ook] of C[ommon] P[rayer] represents the central core—and the continuing doctrinal reference point—of the Anglican tradition of Common Prayer, [the Commission] would want to resist the assumption that the only way to have Common Prayer is to return to the BCP.[13]

—Of course it would want to resist it! The Commission's new position depends crucially on general acceptance of the distinction. Thus do the pirates lay claim to the idea of Common Prayer while allowing us what it is not within their authority to allow or deny us, the Common Prayer

[12] Cited C. W. Kemp, *Faith and Worship* 43, p. 36.
[13] Para. 24, p. 11.

book, the thing itself. It's an audacious stroke, brilliant—except that it is demonstrably disingenuous, the product not of discriminatory thinking but of a predetermined intention to make from the properly indistinguishable a new distinction. For the book is indeed the core, without whose centrality there would be no tradition of Common Prayer; the book is—to borrow the terms of an older debate—*signum exhibitivum* not *signum representativum*.[14] We would however claim too much for the book, as well as too little, if we assented to the Commission's description of it as "the continuing doctrinal reference point": for the book is not a reference point but, with the Ordinal and the Articles, authoritative in a way that neither the ASB nor its replacement could pretend to be.

Words, wrote Taya Zinkin, have an unfortunate habit of imposing themselves and excluding thought. The Commission's manipulation of "Common Prayer" *vis-à-vis* the Common Prayer is a peculiarly wilful form of excluding thought—an exclusion designed to facilitate our deference to the eventual Common [*sic*] Worship.

But what is the Liturgical Commission to do? Clearly, having reinvented the notion of Common Prayer for its own purposes, it can't look back; it must pursue, gripped by its own cliché, the way forward. So it chooses to ignore the challenge mounted in the Prayer Book Society's magazine *Faith and Worship* over several years, and proceeds to assume that its distinction is a real one and widely accepted. Hence the occasion at the Leicester Conference in 1995 when Canon Perham, the Commission's spokesman, said: "You

[14] My borrowing is prompted by Ian Robinson, "Thomas Cranmer on the Real Presence", *Faith and Worship* 43.

understand, don't you, that the Book of Common Prayer and Common Prayer are not exactly the same thing ... ?"— The canon did not wait for an answer, but in due course he got it—in *Faith and Worship*, from Mr Kemp, who in No. 40 described Perham's distinction as part of his "mission of redefinition", his project being "to attach the connotations of old phrases to the denotations of a new scheme".

By 1995 the Liturgical Commission could fairly assume that its act of piracy had worked, that its distinction was understood and approved; for between 1991, when it launched the idea, and 1995, two books had appeared whose titles helped it along: one was called *The Renewal of Common Prayer*,[15] the other *Celebrating Common Prayer*. Of the first Dewi Hopkins remarked (*Faith and Worship* 36) that "it is not what its title suggests", but contends that we should seek "a new understanding of the concept ... an 'evolving common core' of texts varied according to occasion and local culture". Against the second I belatedly pinned a warning label—"no relation" (No. 43). But in the Commission's eyes reiteration of the phrase is enough to justify the assurance: "You understand, *don't* you?"

Perhaps the most subtle of the Commission's depredations on the legitimate tradition is the inclusion of the Book of Common Prayer in bibliographies and acknowledgments, indicating that permission has been sought from the copyright holder. *Celebrating Common Prayer* acknowledges "prayers ... adapted from the Book of Common Prayer, the rights in which are vested in the Crown ..."; a little arrowhead (>) "indicates that minor changes have been made." If I worked for the Crown's Patentee, I would want to inquire

[15] *The Renewal of Common Prayer*, Essays by the Liturgical Commission, ed. Michael Perham.

just what the proposed "minor changes" amounted to—a comma here or there, say? Er, no. The changes are not minor at all but made on the restrictive principle that we address God as "You", and that we sensitively adjust our language to avoid paining the feminists. Unhappily, I have never been in a position to refuse the reprinting of copyright material; so I can only imagine myself responding to the Commission's request in the terms *The Times* laid down for me when I sought to reprint an article by Roger Scruton: yes, provided the article is "reproduced in full with no additions or deletions".

The Sign, a widely circulated parish-magazine inset, published in November 1997 an article by the spokesman for the Liturgical Commission on "the new liturgy", the fruits of the "new scheme" (Kemp). The now familiar distinction between book and idea is repeated, with the assumption that we will endorse the "value" put upon the notion of "common prayer" (note the tactical switch from 1991's upper to 1997's lower case—no doubt to avoid the confusion with the book that earlier must have been found useful). But the Commission now makes this assumption do some rather different work. "If we really believe in common prayer and that a new book [one good new service-book] has more power to unite the church than the old", we should resist any pressure for continued use of the ASB after the year 2000. What an extraordinary position for the pirates to arrive at! The Commission which began by syphoning off the notion of Common Prayer from the book that is our national possession, seeking to "place" the book in the process; which then appropriated the phrase to its own or its friends' publications and tinkered with the text of the Prayer Book; finally turns upon, not the Prayer Book—as the logic of its case requires—but the very book on which its own Alternativism has been built, the poor old ASB, and uses as its instrument a curiously emotive fudge, a sort of blackmail: "If we really believe in common prayer ..." (the conditional clause masking the demand that we all do, or should, or won't want to say we don't).—To which I retort, on behalf of adherents of the ASB, "But I don't: I use the book that was set up, in part at least, in correction of the 'seriously one-sided'[16] Cranmerian Communion service"; and on behalf of Prayer Book adherents, "But you don't, for your belief is in a disembodied notion, a merely clever pretence—by inculcation of which you have come, like Chaucer's Pardoner, finally to deceive yourself—that it has a life independent of the Common Prayer."

And so we arrive at Common Worship, a title withheld even from *The Sign*. The pirates had worked for a decade to claim Common Prayer for their own, ever more wistfully genuflecting towards the phrase; but at the last, fearful of the clouds of critical ridicule gathering above, they settled for ... *Worship*, in the sure and certain hope that their friends in the hymn-book industry would ditch the historic name *Ancient and Modern* and come up, at the right time, with *Common* [sic] *Praise*, plainly designed as a "companion volume" to the "comprehensive" new Prayer Book.

Three points may immediately be made about Common Worship, the achieved artefact, lest Prayer Book adherents be tempted to buy the new book.

(1) The inclusion of parts of 1662 in Common Worship is at best seriously incomplete. At the very heart of the Book of Common Prayer is the Bible, in the form of orderly read-

[16] David Stancliffe's judgement in *Model and Inspiration* (1992).

ing at the Eucharist, at Morning and Evening Prayer throughout the year, and in the monthly saying or singing of every psalm at Morning or Evening Prayer. This principle comes right at the head of Cranmer's reasons for making a new book: it must follow the ancient fathers who

> so ordered the matter that all the whole Bible (or the greatest part thereof) should be read over once every year; intending thereby ... that the people (by daily hearing of holy Scripture read in the Church) might continually profit more and more in the knowledge of God, and be the more inflamed with the love of his true Religion.[17]

Whether the new lectionary is an improvement on any of the Prayer Book lectionaries it is beyond the scope of this essay to inquire, though the most fervent admirers of the former could not claim for it that, as Cranmer claimed for his, it is "plain and easy to be understood". It is at any rate different.

(2) Perhaps next in order of centrality are the collects, the "ultimate examples of Cranmer's genius", as Professor MacCulloch calls them. When the Prayer Book Eucharist is used in the form reprinted in Common Worship *no provision is made for the use of the Prayer Book collects.* Those collects could be imported, but there is no rubric to say so. We are offered a form of the Prayer Book without its most distinctive Prayer.

So the Common Worship version of 1662 will have calendar, lectionary and collects, whether in "traditional" or "contemporary" form, from 1998.

(3) The Bible read will be most unlikely to be the one printed in the Prayer Book as the epistles and gospels. It is

[17] "Concerning the Service of the Church".

already commonplace for recent versions of the Bible to be read in Prayer Book services, and the practice may be expected to become universal in churches using Common Worship, for no edition of the voluminous new Lectionary uses the 1611 Bible.

Even setting aside all questions of the adequacy of, say, the Good News Bible as a translation,[18] it just is nothing to do with the Book of Common Prayer. Common Worship is, like its familiar, *Celebrating Common Prayer*, no relation of Common Prayer.

Well, I have presented the salient facts of the case, as my distrustful, dropping eye beholds them. One more fact, not quite relevant but important in our understanding of the Liturgical Commission, is the fact that the Commission has not once offered to reply to criticisms argued in *Faith and Worship*; and if you read its response to the Prayer Book Society submission (*Faith and Heritage*, Nos. 33–34) you will find no answer to the points made there, merely a series of evasions. I used to think the Commission too secure, or too comfortably aloof, to need to take criticism seriously. I now think that it actually cannot afford to reply to our criticisms. It cannot afford to, I suggest, because it works with one hand tied behind its back—tied by the predetermined principle that we should never address the one God by thou/thee/thy. When we demonstrate (e.g. in *Faith and Worship* 36–39) that by denying ourselves the use of the 2nd person singular we run the grave risk of moving out of the language of prayer into the language of statement and information and commendation (cf. Neil Inkley's line in his

[18] I demonstrate the inaccuracy of the new versions in *Translation* vs *Paraphrase*, in progress. The Good News Bible is more like a downmarket gloss than a translation.

poem in *Faith and Worship* 43: "Not so much of God as the judge of men, as of 'persons' assessing God"), the Commission has no answer: but rather than throw in the towel with an apology for taking up our time, it seeks refuge in an appeal for "friendship", "generosity", "courtesy". If ever there was a classic case of fundamentalism—in the fashionable pejorative sense of the word—drest as principle or commitment, this is it. Understanding the restrictions under which the Commission works, I would be sorry for it—and repent me of my hostility towards it—if it hadn't acquired the powerful position in the church that *The Sign*, representatively, regards as authoritative.

VI
Retrospective Reflections on the Sacred and the Prayer Book

David Martin

Why has the aura of the sacred made the reasoned defence of the Prayer Book so fraught and so difficult, when you might have expected its sacred character to be its "sure defence"? After all, the Prayer Book has been embedded in all those elements of English culture which historically have attracted the sacred into their orbit. It belonged to English time and place and was the most constant lodestone and reference point of English literature, occupying page after page in the *Oxford Book of Quotations*. As George Steiner has commented, even today when we speak planetary English we speak Bible and Prayer Book. When Geza Vermes, another Jew, was asked about what version of the Bible he needed on his Desert Island he chose—after the Hebrew and the Greek texts—the Authorised Version of 1611. How then could the Prayer Book and the Authorised Version be dethroned so easily in the Church whose identity they virtually created and defined? How could it come about that in just one generation it became bad manners, nostalgia and ignorance for the laity to defend what bishops had once lauded as an incomparable liturgy?

For the sociologist it is a serious puzzle and perhaps it is best to begin with the critique which was mounted not so long ago against the very idea of the sacred. Among the proposers of liturgical change were those who sought to abolish the sacred as a sphere marked out and made special in order to carry transcendent meanings. For them it implied two worlds, the mundane and the heavenly, whereas there was in truth only one in which the Holy Spirit of justice and peace was made manifest by Christian action. Perhaps the key word here is action, Christian and otherwise, because the separation of worlds by ritually demarcated borders, such as special gestures, spaces and even consecrated elements, held back "the Kingdom" in some kind of institutional or clerical enclosure. The "man of God" should not be marked off by difference, including the public identity conferred by a collar, but should be out and about in the secular reality. The institutional enclosure of the Church in the course of its modern decline had become too small and its mode of address to God had become a symbol of this confinement, a badge of the static. It was also a reminder of a time when the enclosure served to include rather than to separate. Somehow one had to leap over this wall of separation and *be* in the everyday world, talking its language anonymously alongside everybody else.

By putting it this way I construct a view that rarely had this explicit coherence, but which contributed to an atmospheric. It was an atmospheric with discernible roots in the reduced condition of a Church that had once aimed to "comprehend" a whole population, and of a ministry that had seen itself acting for a people in a place. But that was in the past, and in that past there was the Prayer Book, far from the busy hum of the contemporary market place. Now it was "Goodbye to all that". One would never be in business again until one changed one's address, including address to God. The church building itself as the focus or template of the holy was part of the dualistic theology of separation rather than of "engagement". So some priests were even ready "to deny the temple", because it was the empty and inactive architectural centre of a world that had passed away, literally by-passed and called upon only for incidental trappings and mere ceremony.

The link between past power and glory and contemporary impotence led also to an uncertainty about establishment as yet another source of constriction. Among the proponents of liturgical change were some who also argued for disestablishment, especially if they did not get their way in the ordering of church affairs. They could argue with some justification that the sacred as manifest in the Book of Common Prayer was bound up with regalism and an idea of England in which the Church was an adjunct of a graded society. The life and liberty of the Church depended on a repudiation of everything entailed by patronage, which included, of course, the freedom to revise liturgy so notoriously refused by Parliament in 1928. Autonomy, freedom, revision and renewal were part of the same package; and one should not underestimate the role played by unhappy recollections of the fiasco of 1928 in generating indifference to lay protest over the deposition of the Prayer Book.

There was, maybe, another important factor, to do with the loosening of the tie to the nation. The Book of Common Prayer had been the liturgy of a national Church, but now the "Anglican Communion" was an international body in communication with other such bodies, especially in the world of ecclesiastical bureaucracy. Such bureaucracies build up their own corporate spirit, and the rationale of their existence turns on the making of policy and management of change. In these corridors of ecclesiastical power liturgical change was caught up in the politics of ecumenism, the logic of which implied not the specific Book of Common Prayer but prayers presumed to be held in common between denominations. These were not prayers as actually loved and said, but their revised versions; and it was rashly assumed that the character of Anglicanism resided in a shared spirit not a common text. The argument was that "our unhappy divisions" turned not so much on doctrine as on usage. If people could be weaned away from the distinctive traditions they were used to they would discover they already enjoyed common prayers with other Christians. The obstacle to union lay in what was distinctive, historic and national.

So all kinds of influence tugged at the sacred tie that bound the Church of England to the Book of Common Prayer. Just as in the mid-sixteenth century, a multiplicity of interests bore on the issue of liturgical change which might or might not have to do with reasoned arguments about forms and words. Now in the second half of the twentieth century it was precisely the arrangements then arrived at in terms of the role of monarchy, an independent national church and a reformed vernacular liturgy which had to be undone. This time the multiplicity of interests did not threaten to tear *apart* the state and nation but to tear *away* from both. That meant a transfer of the forum of conflict from the heartland of governance to culture and the inner life of the Church as an increasingly private and voluntary association.

Thus the liturgy of the Church lost its sacred aura through its conversion into a sign of division and focus of cultural contention. Many unspoken differences of attitude and interest could be articulated in relation to the Prayer Book, and translated in terms of the liturgical issue. (One interest which stayed entirely *sotto voce* was economic, in that a great deal had been invested in the production of new books for a near-monopoly market. But that is another story.)

There were other cultural currents inimical to the retention of the Prayer Book, some with interesting theological overtones. One of these was a concern for community, which was presented as a response to contemporary individualism and atomisation. In earlier times there had been a close coincidence of Church and local community and now liturgical reformers hoped for a recovery of organic relationships within a Church set over against a fractured society. A traditional idea of mutuality could be revived in principled contrast to the atomism of "the world". How far this was a practical strategy and how far another example of nostalgia was open to question, given that the main reference points of the everyday existence of Christians lay in work and leisure rather than in the Church. Yet the Prayer Book could be associated with people boxed in on themselves and immobilised in rows of pews: "God's frozen people" as one writer phrased it.

This communitarian impulse in pursuit of fluidity and tangible interaction found expression in numerous ways. Part of the attraction of the Kiss of Peace lay in the opportunity offered to unfreeze people in their private space. They had to be winkled out of their reserve, and incorporated in the wider whole. The revision of Baptism also exemplified this renewed pursuit of tangible community. This required a more explicit incorporation of infants with their families in the body of the Church, and to many people this was in fact genuinely attractive. Yet another expression of community was manifest in the preference for circles and semi-circles over lines and facing east. To stand in a semi-circle around an altar or table allowed direct eye contact and relieved the priest standing at the centre of his sense of isolation. In some of the more charismatic churches the communion of minister and communicant became personal and literally touching. (And yet paradoxically the personal element in individual confession was played down in favour of communal confession, for reasons to be suggested later.)

What served to legitimate these varied changes was the appeal to primitive practice. This was how things were ordered in the springtime of the Church and maybe their revival would in turn revive contemporary Christians. The scholarship which suggested that the "westward position" was primitive or that the text of the Creed took the form of a communal "we" rather than a personal "I" might be very debateable but the changes proposed felt right in terms of the Zeitgeist of the sixties. Those who opposed these shifts were not only for stasis against dunamis but attached to the letter of Cranmer when they ought truly to emulate his reforming spirit.

The spirit of the sixties also militated against order and ceremony. The priest therefore sought to encourage informality, talking a congregation through the service, rather than circumspection in "the people's" approach to the sacred. The reverence once thought due to the transcendent located in the holy place needed to be dissolved in the fellow-feeling of a divine immanence potentially located anywhere. So while the transcendent God had been addressed with due reverence through invocation and evocation, the immanent God present in all things needed to be addressed in ordinary speech. Whereas "thou" implied difference and even distance "you" implied sharing, cooperation and proximity.

The objection to formality included an objection to form as embodied in shared texts known by heart. One Roman Catholic bishop actually declared he took active steps to avoid the kind of repetition that led to knowing something by heart. In this (as in so many other ways) the assumptions of ecclesiastical reformers mirrored those of educational reformers. According to the traditional approach you extended your understanding through learning by rote what you only half-apprehended. Repetition was the pathway to appropriation, and only when something was automatic could you reflect and monitor what had been incised in the tablets of the heart. Acquisition was embedded in resonance. According to the alternative approach you were introduced not so much to texts as to notions, and the forms might vary as much as you liked provided you picked up the idea. Form and substance were disjoined as part of a wider and exaggerated pursuit of inwardness. Inevitably, this rendered irrelevant the issue of a memorable text, and in practice revision blurred memory through the sheer proliferation of alternatives. And yet, if one considers the classical form of the sermon, it depends to a high degree on resonances stirred up through the creative rearrangement of mosaics of quotation. The sermon was a "recalling to mind", not by reference to evanescent notions but by recollection of a common text and a common prayer. You "read, mark, learn and inwardly digest," in that order.

The sharpest focus for this loose ensemble of attitudes was provided by the idea of unworthiness before God. This has somehow become confused with complaints about "low self-esteem" but it is part of the diminution in the distance between God and Man which in an extreme form stressed the divinisation of the human. Reformers wished to remove too grave a sense of the enormity of sin and of deprecation or prostration before the divine majesty. It no longer made sense to say with Isaiah "Woe is me for I am a man of unclean lips and I dwell among a people of unclean lips." In fact the "people of God" were well-intentioned citizens whose understandable mistakes represented just the kind of poor judgement capable of redress by decent counselling. Evil was little more than "unacceptable behaviour", mildly "out of order", as if the twentieth century were not the century of Auschwitz, Cambodia and Rwanda.

Here the political edge was at its sharpest because the communal emphasis shifted responsibility from one's own sin to the structural maladjustments maintained by collective agencies. Whatever "I" personally might have done was in the context of what an impersonal "they" had brought about. Righteousness lay not so much in the merciful compassion of the Lord as in blame attributed to maleficent collective others. Individual freewill and personal responsibility were swallowed up in a collective constraint which rendered the individual more victim than agent. Actually the logic of political rectitude in due course reversed this because it implied that the collective victims "out there" lacked creativity and agency, but there still remained a residue of unease about taking personal responsibility for misdeeds. The preference for collective rather than personal confession lay in this band of feeling.

Whatever the merits of all this (and after all few of us under duress refuse to take advantage of psycho-social escape clauses) it made for excuse rather than confession, victimage rather than expiation or "amendment of life". It is perhaps an instance of what Blake meant when he said that "Damn braces and bless relaxes". The Prayer Book shared precisely this kind of bracing realism about human potential by going beyond decency and unhappy misunderstanding to culpability and redemption. It provided no easeful synonyms for sin.

The other side of refusing to plumb the depths of our abasement was an accent on "celebration". There were many attractive aspects to this: the sense of God's gifts and our own response, a rejoicing in the bountiful fruits of creation, a joy in the meal shared out in justice to every creature and in the fellowship of the forgiven, but there was an unease about the sacrificial cost exacted by evil as the price of atonement. This was evident not so much in the wording of the revised texts (though the new Roman collects were often banal in their childish Pelagianism) as in reservations about the old ones. It was true that the old texts could imply a substitutionary understanding of the atonement whereby the wrath of an offended father was deflected by the pre-determined and innocent suffering of his son, but what the Prayer Book unequivocally set forth was the full costing of evil. We have recourse not to our own righteousness but to the divine mercy, placarded before us in the cross of Christ. For the Prayer Book *Crux probat omnia*. We are not mainly celebrating solidarity in communion, but our redemption through the blood of Christ.

Celebration had other aspects bearing on the extremely difficult question of the aesthetic in worship which was rarely debated with proper seriousness. Those who defended the

Prayer Book sometimes appealed to the way the holiness of beauty can complement the beauty of holiness. It is a respectable argument, used by defenders of church music against an earlier cohort of Puritans, though probably not one which would have appealed to Cranmer. But it led revisers to complain their critics were mainly moved by aesthetic considerations, as well as by preference for the familiar and archaic. At the same time, they themselves were oddly inconsistent both as to the aesthetic and the archaic. Perhaps some of this stemmed from a McLuhanite analysis about a shift from the verbal to the visual and tangible. That implied a treatment of words from a functional perspective, reducing the poetic (and especially poetic redundancy) to the utilitarian, informing people about God rather than addressing him, while seeking aesthetic impact through the decorative arts. Indeed, so far as vestments were concerned, the revisers turned quite sportive. So whereas the verbal ikon was stripped down, the visual icon was enhanced.

Music lay somewhere between the verbal and the visual, since you simply cannot strip down resonance where music is concerned. Music refuses to be information about God or information offered to God. What tended to happen with respect to music was a penchant for modest imitations of popular rhythms, just enough to differentiate the product from the slow, square and solemn mode of traditional hymnody. Again, this mirrored changes in the schools where access to traditional hymnody was virtually cut off in favour of jog-trot ditties. Though poetic redundancy might be frowned upon in liturgical prose it flourished mightily in the repetitions of the new sacred song.

On all these matters it was virtually impossible to join serious debate in a common forum on shared ground because the potential parties to discussion had incommensurate frames of reference. For one thing the revisers saw themselves as charged with a sacred task whereas the critics simply deployed the content of their professional expertise, whether literary, sociological or whatever. When in the mid-eighties I asked whether well known Christian academics might meet with members of the liturgical commission I was told they "were not ready for that". Similarly, when Rachel Trickett, Principal of St Hugh's, Oxford, did address some of those concerned in implementation of liturgical change she was greeted with uncomprehending hostility. It was simply improper to subject sincere efforts undertaken for the good of the Church to these external and professional criteria. This, after all, was the way the Church was going and it was a matter of "tools for the job". At the local level the new tools could be promoted by a mixture of chivvying and cozenage, so this kind of detailed debate was unsettling, particularly since the kinds of scholarship deployed were so different.

And yet some of the issues were simple and obvious, such as the likely consequences of trying to alter the Lord's Prayer. The technical issues of retranslation were very complex, but the result would clearly be confusion worse confounded, as different versions were promoted and people at large and outside the churches lost access to their only "common prayer". As the great hymns were relegated (or made unfamiliar by revision) so, too, the Lord's Prayer ceased to be a shared possession.

An equally obvious issue turned on whether or not the new "tools for the job" would have any impact on the diminishing appeal of the Church. Though it might subsequently be denied that this was a major motive for change, in fact this was precisely how the proposed revisions were presented to local congregations. Characteristically, they would be asked to cooperate in an "experiment" which would help the Church communicate more effectively with the contemporary world, especially young people. And this argument was by far the most effective because it encouraged those otherwise reluctant, to sacrifice their own predilections to secure the survival of their Church. At Guildford Cathedral, for example, the diocesan addressed the congregation in 1997 in precisely these terms, arguing that they had no future unless they changed.

The argument was in essence sociological and as such implausible to a degree. So far as I was concerned, work on the processes of secularization over three decades and more attributed little if anything in the process of decline to the impact of the linguistic register. The social changes separating the Church from a post-Christian culture were such that tinkering with language could make not the slightest difference to ecclesiastical survival rates. Yet to articulate the obvious was to intrude an inadmissible mode of secular argument into sacred space. In any case, it was too depressing to be countenanced. The hard-pressed priest faced with apathy understandably needed to believe that changes of this kind would make a difference. Their irrelevance was psychologically unsustainable.

Intrusion on sacred space and on the unction that characteristically governs discourse in sacred *milieux* provides a major reason why the academic critique failed to make contact, along with the way in which the linguistic issue served to channel several other issues. That immediately directs attention to the priestly guardians of sacred space as those who were ultimately in control of the local agenda. After all, whoever controls the agenda (and writes the minutes) on a day-to-day basis effectively determines what happens, whatever the course of debate. Naturally priests or ministers regard the "sharp end" of a church as their sphere of operations and indeed the place where a life's work is undertaken. In an increasingly secular society it is a last defensible redoubt, after other forms of public role have been successively relinquished. No matter that the laity was supposed to participate under the new rubrics, in practice the only participation offered was symbolic. Priests determined the conditions of their own labour. If the vicar calls the new "material" contemporary language then one doesn't ask just who in the contemporary world speaks in that peculiar way.

There were many elements at work here. One should never, for example, underestimate the itch for change generated by boredom, and the sense that the clerical profession ought to change in the same way as other professions. Again, whereas lay persons wanted a service the priest might well envisage the eucharist as a vehicle for the various communitarian and other concerns discussed earlier. Above all, the style of church governance now combined the guardianship of the sacred (and the unction governing that role) with contemporary management (and the language that brings in its train). What still remained inadmissible was a democratic space for rational disagreement. Relationships of charisma and discipleship and the expository mode simply do not admit that. Everybody understands it is a form of discourtesy intruded into the holy place, and where so many other issues of cultural disagreement lie waiting in the wings that is at all costs to be avoided.

Priests and ministers are not the only guardians of the sacred, and issues of liturgical change immediately throw into relief the comparative conservatism of those who in practice make ritual performance possible. What the verger or crucifer does in sacred space is a wholly satisfying privilege, and he or she enjoys knowing "the ritual reason why" and acting by the book. Service is embedded in minutiae which protect the character of ritual action, rendering it efficacious. The sign works in its use and is undermined by explaining what it is supposed to do. The automatic response which is the basis of this kind of satisfaction can afford to be implicit without the distractions of commentary. Yet the views of these key participants are never called for: they, of all people, are not invited to comment on what most nearly concerns them.

In trying to set out the problems encountered in the earlier cycle of liturgical change it has not been my role to comment directly on the Book of Common Worship introduced in 2000. The new generation of revisers by including so much of the Prayer Book clearly recognises how much was lost in the deposition of the common text. For that I, for one, am grateful, though remaining sceptical about the local politics whereby change is still promoted, knowing only too well how these matters are often managed. My object in this article has been simply to suggest clues about what has happened, in the context of "the sacred". These clues are the slow withdrawal of the Church, willed or not, from a national role, the cultural preoccupations of the sixties, and the activities of national and international bureaucracies, especially regarding the high politics of ecumenism. Then there was a poorly focussed feeling that *something* had to be done. Throughout a long and sorry history the umbrella of the sacred was extended to prevent the serious debate that ought to have been conducted, forcing frustration into angry protest and, in many cases, slow and disappointed disengagement. Liturgical change could have been accomplished without discontinuity or deposition and displacement. Somehow, for some of the reasons suggested, that simply did not happen.

VII
The Question of Style[1]

Ian Robinson

To the best of our knowledge human beings are the only mortal creatures who talk, a not unmixed blessing which some associate with the fall into the knowledge of good and evil. That fatal step goes beyond the animal kingdom. The likelihood must be that if the rabbits could talk they would be sinners.

Whosoever shall call upon the name of the Lord shall be saved. To do that, we have to be granted the grace to call, and we have to have the Name revealed to us. The redemptive process of Christianity, the reconciling the world to God, is amongst other things a redemption of language. In language we see the world in lights different from any available to the other animals. We believe that Christ is the true light. "Fallen, fallen light renew" is part of the Church's mission. The individual is enabled by the redeemed language to call upon God; but, because in language, not privately. Salvation is always of the individual but never private-and-personal, for it is the entry into the Body of Christ.

It is still necessary, half a century after Eliot and Leavis, Wittgenstein and Collingwood, to repeat that language is

[1] Parts of this essay derive from three publications in *Faith and Worship*.

more than the dress of thought. "How we clothe this essential movement [Godwards] in the words which articulate it is the proper task of liturgical texts," explains the present chairman of the Liturgical Commission.[2] But we don't first have the naked movement then clothe it, and if we did there would be no advantage in the clothed over the naked. And the style, the *how*, affects any *what* of what is said. Whatever made the poet begin the well-known elegy on Queen Victoria with the time-honoured words "Dust to dust, ashes to ashes," his style ensured that what actually happened was not elegy, when he continued, "Into the tomb the great Queen dashes"—not elegy because not made in language.

There cannot be a good liturgy with a bad style, though it is possible to have a bad liturgy with a good style, which in a nutshell was what Dix thought of Cranmer—good in the sense of making something in language with deep clarity, bad because Dix thought he should have been making something else.

The great drive behind the stylistic upheavals of the last half century has been the feeling that if the gospel is to be proclaimed in the modern world it must be in that world's language, not in the archaic, hard-to-understand language of Cranmer. There is already a difficulty here if the gospel has to be in but not of the world. The word can only possibly be preached in the act of redeeming language. This is what our Lord himself and the apostles and writers of the New Testament did for Greek,[3] Jerome for Latin, what the translators of the New Testament and of the Psalms into Old English did in their time, and the compilers of the Book of Common Prayer in theirs. And the compilers of

[2] David Stancliffe, *Model and Inspiration*, 1993, p. 19.

[3] Or Aramaic, if you wish, but cf. G. R. Selby, *Jesus, Aramaic and Greek*, Brynmill Press, 1989.

The Alternative Service Book 1980 in theirs? Somehow the analogy will not work.

The functional importance of style was not sufficiently understood in the years of experimentation that led to the New English Bible and then to the ASB. It was assumed rather simply that there is no great difficulty in presenting the gospel in the language of the day. The Prayer Book could be expected to fade away as intelligible everyday speech attracted people back into the newly filled churches. If this were possible, only Antichrist could resist it. Somehow, though, the programme seems not to be working well. Christianity is not more generally known in this country than it was forty years ago. The churches are not any fuller; on the contrary. The language of the media is not more Christian.

I suggest that the first reason for the mixed fortunes of the modern liturgies is that their language is not genuinely contemporary, if by that is meant more like common speech than the Prayer Book and more generally intelligible.

Complimenting the Prince of Wales on the "brave and good thing" he did when agreeing to become patron of the Prayer Book Society, *The Daily Telegraph* commented,

> There are some bishops, and a great many parish priests, who would cheerfully see [the Book of Common Prayer] consigned for ever to the archives. They much prefer to address their creator in the more modern, colloquial language of the *Alternative Service Book*.[4]

It is taken for granted by this wide-awake newspaper in the act of defending the Prayer Book that the language of ASB is more modern and colloquial which, after all, would be

[4] 7 March 2000, p. 31.

expected of a book published in 1980. During the composition of its successor, Common Worship, "A decision was taken at an early stage to render all the Prayer Book collects into contemporary liturgical language... it was recognized that, in churches where the language of worship is almost exclusively contemporary, there was a need for the collects to conform to the norm," Dean Perham tells us.[5] But the question what liturgical revisers understand by "contemporary", not discussed by Dean Perham, is not straightforward, for neither ASB nor Common Worship is in fact written in what anyone outside the Church would think of as contemporary, "modern, colloquial" language. Take "colloquial" to mean "what would not stand out as unusual in conversation" and imagine anyone saying, anywhere but in church, "hallowed", still there in the "contemporary" Lord's Prayer, or "Hosanna in the Highest!"[6] Or imagine anyone using the word *glory* on any occasion without trying to make anyone smile. At the presentation of Oscars, say, or to a National Lottery winner, or the knighting of a pop-star: "Earth, Sir Elton, is full of your glory."[7] (What would the genuinely modern phrase be? There's your glitz, man, all over Planet Earth?) If this is modern, colloquial, or exclusively contemporary language of worship, what does it exclude? Not, evidently, some very old words and phrases heard nowhere else.

Once notice that some phrases even in ASB are far from any other English, and you may also begin to notice that the speciality is very common. "Blood of the new covenant" is a phrase used in Eucharistic Prayer 8 of the new Order One, the prayer which we are told is designed to be understood by eight-year-olds. We, though not eight-year-olds, do meet

[5] Michael Perham, *Celebrate the Christian Story*, 1997, p. 38.
[6] ASB Rite A, the "modern language" rite, p. 134, and Common Worship Order 1, p. 28.
[7] *Ibid.*

covenants outside church: legal and taxation documents, though not nowadays signed in blood. But nobody would use this phrase on "Any Questions", because it would be deemed either unintelligible, or archaic, or special, or all three.

A few more examples.

English even in its inflected days never had a vocative case; from early Middle English a formal address to a person was often instead made by "O" followed by the nominative, in what the Dictionary calls the "vocative relation". This is said to be a use of the "exclamation, expressive of feeling" still common, but the quasi-vocative use is now distinct. The two are often though not always distinguished by spelling the exclamation with an *h*, as in "Oh, John, *please* shut the door," which "Oh!" is an independent interjection, usually exasperated or longsuffering, not a vocative. In *Paradise Lost* Adam and Eve occasionally begin addressing one another with an "O", as when Adam, hearing the dreadful news of Eve's fall, begins with "O fairest of creation ... "[8] but it is not to be expected in modern family conferences.

This form of address, though there is no difficulty in understanding it, is in fact completely disused in contemporary colloquial English, except in the comic, prayer-derived exclamation "O my gawd!", and has been for ages. Shakespeare was already making jokes about it in the heavy apostrophizing of the night and the wall in the play of Pyramus and Thisby: "And thou O wall, O sweet, O lovely wall ... ."[9] Lewis Carroll continued the joke when Alice addresses the Mouse:

"O Mouse, do you know the way out of this pool? I am

[8] *Paradise Lost* IX. 896.
[9] *A Midsummer Night's Dream* V. i.

> very tired of swimming about here, O Mouse!" (Alice thought this must be the right way of speaking to a mouse: she had never done such a thing before, but she remembered having seen in her brother's Latin Grammar, "A mouse—of a mouse—to a mouse—a mouse—O mouse!")[10]

Quite a number of the collects in Common Worship, though not in ASB, begin with "O".[11] So the return to "O" as a common beginning for a collect is deliberate archaism. The remarkable thing is that, four hundred years after Shakespeare's jokes and more than a century after Lewis Carroll's, it is also so natural as to need an effort to notice. But how is "O" supposed to be contemporary if we never hear it outside church?

Is "grant" ever used in non-religious modern English as a verb? Perhaps in rather old-fashioned phrases like "I grant you that" and of course in the participle "taken for granted". But the imperative? The new Ascension Day collect begins "Grant . . .". Has this archaism raised a storm of protest from them that want a contemporary liturgy?

Even ASB addresses God frequently as "Lord". The House of Lords is still so called, but the word is hardly ever used to ordinary human lords, and even when it is, the phrase is always "my lord", never used to God. Christianity can't do without "lord" any more than the equally special "saviour". "Lord" in this use goes back to our roots in the Psalms and the Old Testament ways of addressing God. In the days of the temple sacrifices His name was a dreadful secret, to be used only once in the year by the High Priest in the Holy of Holies. Instead of the great and terrible Name,

[10] *Alice in Wonderland*, Chapter II, "The Pool of Tears".
[11] The word is used infrequently in ASB, for instance in the opening versicle of Morning Prayer, p. 49.

they called Him Adonai, the LXX *kurios*, which in English has always been the Lord, on whom we call. There is no other word for "lord" any more than "Christ". (Even if we got more literal and started using "Anointed" that would need notes and naturalization and would still itself be special.)

The people are invited to respond with an "Amen" to many prayers, a word used outside church only in jokes.

A "contemporary" prayer, then, can begin "Grant, O Lord ..." and end "through Jesus Christ our lord, Amen." "Through", too, is used in a sense special to prayer. This means that in these phrases the *only* word used in an ordinary contemporary sense is "our". Such is the "exclusively contemporary" language of the Church of England.

If Radio 4 News bulletins are what is understood by "modern, colloquial" English, any claim that new liturgies are modern or colloquial is sheer bluff. The bluff's other face declares that the Prayer Book is now unintelligible because of its archaic English, a belief behind the most serious demands for modernization, but one that is equally untenable.[12] The Prayer Book does not talk down to the congregation, but the parts meant to be spoken by the congregation are models of plainness. Whether the Liturgical Commission has ever taken the precaution of organizing polls about what can and what cannot be understood I do not know. It is quite clear, anyway, that modern liturgical work is not more generally comprehensible than the Prayer Book. Nor is it (as Bishop Stancliffe seems to think[13]) more inclined to monosyllables. The oftenest used confession in the Prayer Book says, with one disyllable in these thirty-one

[12] *Élitism* is a word almost as hard to use untendentiously as *sexism* or *racism*; but is not this a form of it? The clergy did not themselves think the Prayer Book's language difficult, only too difficult for *us*.

[13] "Simple words should be preferred to more complex ... ." (*Model and Inspiration*, 1993, p. 20).

monosyllables, "We have left undone those things which we ought to have done, and we have done those things which we ought not to have done, and there is no health in us." Could anyone with any smattering of English fail to understand that?—provided only that the word *ought* is a real part of their vocabulary. It is true that the same confession calls for an understanding of mercy and penitence. So must any Christian confession. Is it the words that are difficult or the whole mode of thought? ASB/Common Worship equivalent:

> We have sinned...
> through negligence, through weakness,
> through our own deliberate fault.[14]

The difficulty that the (wo)man in the street may have is with *any* language of Christianity, "to the Greeks foolishness". *Sin* is no easier to understand in the language of the media than *oblation*. Is *love* itself generally comprehensible in the sense understood by Christians? (Thomas Hardy thought love is a *feeling*!) There are very important questions about what any religious language can mean in public at the present day, but they apply equally to the Prayer Book, the Alternative Service Book 1980 and Common Worship.

If ASB/Common Worship are intelligible at all to the unchurched masses it is by way their indebtedness to the traditional language, principally of the English Bible and the Book of Common Prayer, which still to some extent permeates common life.

When modern liturgists claim to be using exclusively contemporary language and the papers think of it as modern and colloquial I have to ask, then, the old question, *Who*

[14] Common Worship has replaced "negligence" with "ignorance", thereby introducing another polysyllable and the question much discussed by theologians whether it is possible to sin in ignorance.

is kidding whom about what? To be sure, Dean Perham's phrase about the collects was not "contemporary English" but "contemporary liturgical language". If the phrasing was deliberate, "contemporary liturgical language" is tacitly defined by contrast with other liturgical language, not with whatever else is contemporary; which does appear to be the case. What the modern liturgies give us is not a contemporary, intelligible language of worship, but modifications of ordinary religious English.

In fact, whatever is said, and however sincerely, by liturgical revisers, the effort to be contemporary was never realistic and is now being quietly abandoned. The present Liturgical Commission has decided that it is no enemy of tradition, which could hardly be the case if the initial demands for modern language were right. For if new language is necessary to get the Word spoken in the modern world it just is, and that's that.

The Commission's new kindlier attitude to the Prayer Book has taken two principal forms. Firstly, much of the Prayer Book is incorporated into Common Worship. The 1662 eucharist is reprinted, though not quite straightforwardly, as we have seen and shall see; and 1662 Morning and Evening Prayer will co-exist (peacefully, the Commissioners hope) with new productions. Moreover, to complete the set of options, both an "Order One in Traditional Language" and "Order Two in Contemporary Language" are printed, so that we can choose the Prayer Book Holy Communion without its language or the revised Rite A using "thou". So the Prayer Book itself comes into the new book, on equal terms with the new writing. As a member of the Prayer Book Society I am happy to be able to welcome this, whatever reservations follow.

The second principal movement towards something more traditional is seen most conspicuously in the style of the collects newly composed for Common Worship, which are less "contemporary" than, shall we say, the bare version of the Gloria in Excelsis in the 1980 Rite A, though that survives in the new Order One.

If the gratitude a "traditionalist" feels for the concessions to the Prayer Book is not unqualified, he is sure to be seen as the dangerous animal biting the kindly keeper's hand as it tries to feed him, under the mistaken impression that once again *on l'attaque*. But the question how well the new liturgical work, of either the 1980 or the 2000 style, succeeds as modification of the old is thrust on us by its relation to the old. And if the new is so dependent on the old we may go as far as asking why change is thought necessary at all. It will at first glance seem churlish to say, for instance, that the new collects are no more "traditional" than the collects of the ASB, and in some ways more objectionable, because even further, at the same time, from English speech. Truth, however, will out, and such, I am afraid, is the case.

Before we glance at the "you" English, prominent in these collects, that the Liturgical Commission evidently takes to be the central departure from tradition, let us take the small-looking example of the use of "may" in absolutions and blessings.

Blessings and curses in English are made with a kind of iussive subjunctive. The subjunctive is the grammatical mood otherwise associated with conditional existence, with possibility or desire rather than actuality. As with many other bits of English the subjunctive can be formed with auxiliaries ("All may yet be well", "Hoping it might be so"); but it also has its simple form as in "Long live the King!" In "Zadok the Priest" two subjunctives lead to a "periphrastic" subjunctive formed with the auxiliary *may*: "God save the King; long live the King; may the King live for ever!" There the longer third phrase has a rhetorical point; but the auxiliary forms with *may* or *might* are normally weaker though less ambiguous than the straight subjunctive. The latter comes, for instance, three times, immediately after the opening address to the Father in the commonest prayer, before it goes over to imperatives [15] and the indicative of the doxology. "Hallowed be thy Name. Thy kingdom come. Thy will be done ...". The professedly contemporary version of ASB and Common Worship retains the form,

> hallowed be your name,
> your kingdom come,
> your will be done.

"May your kingdom come" would be a decided come-down. *God bless you!* is stronger than *May God bless you!* Why should this be?

Jespersen remarks on the use in modern English of the same form of the verb for infinitive, imperative, subjunctive and much of the present indicative.[16] "These may therefore be considered various functions of the same form," he says—not just coincidental identities. It is making a very fine distinction to say that *So be it* is subjunctive not imperative. Think how slight the difference is between "God save the king!" (subjunctive) and "O Lord, save the Queen" (impera-

[15] Some grammarians use the term *precative* for the petitions of prayer, presumably because *imperative* suggests commands and it is thought improper to give orders to God. Any English "precatives" are formally identical with the imperative, and I shall use this as the more ordinary term.
[16] Otto Jespersen, *Essentials of English Grammar*, 1933, p. 293.

tive); "God grant ... " (subjunctive), only a comma away from "God, grant ... " (imperative). According to the Folio, Edmund's climactic prayer is, "Now Gods, stand up for bastards."[17] The comma-pause does make it a prayer. Without the comma it would be a subjunctive from the sense, though it could equally be taken as indicative: "various functions of the same form".

This imperative-indicative-infinitive-subjunctive is peculiarly primitive and naked. I think the subjunctives overlap with other uses of the verb stem not only formally but semantically. This would be good Saussurean linguistics: if there is no *différence*, the subjunctive forms may give simultaneous hints of indicative or imperative or infinitive, whereas *may* unambiguously utters a wish and nothing else. May the best man win!—but he may not. It is not fanciful to suppose that poets and liturgists make use of the overlap of forms.

> Jesus shall reign where'er the sun
> Doth his successive journeys run;
> His kingdom stretch from shore to shore ....

Reign and *run* are stems or infinitives after different auxiliaries (the *shall* used prophetically to make more than a simple future), and grammatically I suppose *stretch* is another infinitive after the *shall* of line one. But the identity of forms gives a phrase that also suggests a subjunctive. This has the effect of including a "let it be" sense as well as "it shall be." "Blessings abound where'er he reigns" is presumably indicative but would be unchanged as subjunctive, with the force of "Let blessings abound ... ".

The periphrastic *may, could, should* forms are not suggest-

[17] *King Lear* I. ii. 22; Shakespeare First Folio, facsimile edn. ed. Kökeritz, New Haven, 1955, p. 776.

ive like this. "Thy lips rot off!" says someone in Shakespeare's *Timon of Athens*. Shakespeare would never have written "May thy lips rot off!" because, I am suggesting, the *may* removes the simultaneous presence of imperative and, in that case, indicative, for the sentence would have exactly the same words in the same order, though possibly different stress or intonation, if it were indicative meaning *thy lips are rotting off*. The identity of forms makes that subjunctive express, as well as a wish, a wish-fulfilment.

"God be merciful to us and bless us": the *be* is not as explicit as the *may* of a wish or the *is* of the "copula" which asserts, propositionally, connection or identity. As well as a wish and a prayer this *be* is actually a verbal creation of blessing, a kind of enactment of its being. It is quite close to what Austin called performatives, words that perform an action rather than describe, like *I bet*, *I promise* or in the marriage service "I *N* take thee *N*. . . ." The use of the words in the proper circumstances makes the marriage.[18] When the Bishop says "The Lord bless you and keep you," he *is* uttering a wish and also a prayer that is close to those other odd forms using *let*; but I believe that there is simultaneously a linguistic *deed*, namely a blessing. The whole has what Austin called *illocutionary force*, something accomplished in language; whereas with "May" we have only a sort of hankering after a blessing.

ASB did not use the form "May the blessing of God almighty . . . ", though we must all have heard it many times. Common Worship adopts it, for instance, at just a moment when one would hope for some more definite reassurance, the end of communion for the dying:

[18] Cf. J. L. Austin, *How to Do Things with Words*, Oxford, 1962, and my discussion in *The New Grammarians' Funeral*, Cambridge, 1975, pp. 107–11.

> May the eternal God
> bless and keep us . . . .[19]

This is an invitation to remember that in actual speech *may* often expresses wishful thinking, as when Claudius says "All may yet be well."

A *may* in an absolution is the same let-down. The new Compline in Traditional Language has an optional absolution:

> *A priest may say*
> May the almighty and merciful Lord
> grant unto you pardon and remission of all your sins . . . .

The repetition of the word *may* from rubric to absolution makes my point. *May* cannot sound like the Prayer Book's "power and commandment to declare and pronounce to his people, being penitent, the absolution and remission of their sins". *May* has, again, the force of "I hope everything is going to be all right": which is not absolution. Contrast, from 1662,

> Almighty God . . . Have mercy upon you; pardon and deliver you from all your sins; confirm and strengthen you in all goodness; and bring you to everlasting life; through Jesus Christ our Lord. *Amen.*

These are all subjunctives, but it would be diluting the Prayer Book's theology to say that they only express a wish. The use of the single subjunctive/imperative form is much more naturally performative, expressing the actual remission of sins.

The 1662 indicative at the Morning and Evening Prayer absolution is another matter: I think it is a form not re-

[19] *Liturgical Material Commended by the House of Bishops*, GS Misc 594, 2000, p. 20.

corded by grammarians. "He pardoneth and absolveth", unambiguously indicative, is not a report of a fact but something actually occurring at that moment, like "with this ring I thee wed". The (grammatically) unusual thing is the third person; performatives are more ordinarily first. The theology is, of course, sound: it is God who pardons; but that is what is happening at that moment.

In the Lord's Prayer, the simple subjunctives do more than wish. They do hallow the Name; they align the will of the congregation with the divine will as a sort of *amen*, or as in the French subjunctive *soit*, so that the coming of the Kingdom is at least momentarily something being done, not just willed.

The *may* forms are "contemporary" in making a contrast with traditional language. It is a contrast that is bound to heighten the feebleness of the new forms. A preacher who begins a sermon, as I expect we have all heard more than once, "May my words be in the Name of God," has followed the weakness to the point of grammatical incongruity. That the words are in the Name is just something declared, not something wished that may or may not be the case. Whether they are fit to be uttered in the name of God is another question, but here *may* is like a stage policeman thundering on the door and saying "May your opening be in the name of the Law!" or a juryman trying to take the oath by saying "May I swear . . . ." This is unlike the well-known "May the words of my mouth . . . be always acceptable in thy sight", which can indeed express a suitable hopeful humility, recognizing the possibility that they may not be.

Dean Perham's leading example of exclusively contemporary language was the collects, and "exclusively contemporary" here refers to the refusal to use either the second person singular or a certain kind of relative clause. The "*Guidelines on Language*" in *Patterns for Worship*, 1989, tell those "writing their own material" to do so "without a string of dependent clauses", to "avoid complicated sentence constructions" and "keep sentences as short as possible. Use full stops rather than semicolons." These are guidelines not arguments and so we are left to imagine why we should not use complex sentences. The fourth of the guidelines is very obedient to the guidelines, being four words long: "Address God as you."[20] Again, we are not told why. Nobody will go to the stake for "thou", we were told a few years ago.[21] This is rather odd of a matter to which the Liturgical Commission evidently attaches great importance. Let us ask, anyway, what difference it makes when these principles are adopted.

ASB Ninth Sunday (or sixty-odd shopping days) Before Christmas had a collect beginning:

> Almighty God,
> you have created the heavens and the earth
> and made man in your own image.

This short compound sentence correctly ends with a full stop, which if this were an ordinary conversation would suggest a pause for a reply. ("Oh yes! so I did! Thank you for reminding me.") The difference from such things in older prayers as "Thou art the king of glory, O Christ!" in the Te Deum or "For thou only art holy" in the Gloria in Excelsis is that they are genuine exclamations of praise and wonder; whereas the short indicative sentences of the new collects are just statements.

[20] *Patterns for Worship*, p. 273.
[21] Cf. A. C. Capey's editorial in *Faith and Worship*, Summer, 2000.

Their use is explained, though not excused, by their origin. As I explained in a recent book, among the many reasons why Cranmer's collects are of great historical importance is their naturalization in English of the complex sentence, and with it, to a remarkable degree, a modern world.[22] The normal pattern in Cranmer's collects, firmly established in English in 1549, was to work any "information" into a relative clause, which makes it an *aide mémoire* to ourselves, not God. We remind ourselves of the attribute of God relevant to the petition, but in the (syntactic) context of addressing Him: as against making a new main clause to remind Him of what He presumably knows better than we do. The insistence on asyndeton produces the latter oddity. Its frequency in ASB has been subjected to much criticism during the twenty years of the book's use.[23]

Common Worship has learned the lesson, but only to the extent of using colons instead of the ASB's full points. This is certainly an improvement, in that it makes us aware that the information is pointing to something that follows. But whether the major punctuation separating main clauses is a full point or a colon is a rhetorical not a syntactic matter. Whether these formations will be read as if they are one sentence is dubious. Next Ash Wednesday, for instance, some will hear:

> Almighty and everlasting God
> you hate nothing that you have made
> and forgive the sins of all those who are penitent:
> create and make in us new and contrite hearts ....

This is identical with ASB except that ASB has a full point at the end of line three and then starts a new sentence. By

[22] Cf. Ian Robinson, *The Establishment of Modern English Prose*, Cambridge, 1998.
[23] Cf. for instance above p. 24, and *Private Eye*'s long-running series of extracts from the Rocky Horror Service Book.

the colon Common Worship is trying to bring the syntax closer to the Prayer Book's relative clause subordinate to the main verb "create"; but the ASB full point is syntactically more honest. Common Worship would have been much improved had the revisers learnt the lesson of the Prayer Book and incorporated the *protasis* into the same syntactic structure as the petition. The new text needs the substitution of one phoneme, to read "who hate" instead of "you hate". Why was this not done? The volume of the new collects "in traditional language" uses these second person relatives as a matter of course, so that the Ash Wednesday collect just quoted is retranslated into a form that will be familiar to some:

> Almighty and everlasting God,
> who hatest nothing that thou hast made
> and dost forgive the sins of all them that are penitent:
> create and make in us new and contrite hearts . . . .

The only cavil there is that a comma would have been better than the colon, which obscures the point that we are inside one syntactic structure not two. So why can we not have these relative clauses in the second person plural "contemporary"? Strange that the sense of the contemporary includes forms as odd and unnatural sounding as the information-presenting indicative, but excludes these!

Common Worship does allow, quite frequently, relative clauses with a past tense. The Third Sunday of Advent collect begins, "O Lord Jesus Christ, / who at your first coming sent . . . " before going on to a main-clause "grant . . . ." The one for the Fourth Sunday of Advent begins "God our redeemer, / who prepared the Blessed Virgin Mary . . . " before in its turn continuing to "grant . . . ." But for

Christmas Eve, when we might expect "Almighty God, who make us glad ..." and Christmas Day, "Almighty God, who have given us ..." we get instead, "Almighty God, / you make us glad ..." and "Almighty God, / you have given us ... ." I spotted one that uses the perfect, though with the verb separated from the pronoun: "Almighty God, / who through your only begotten son Jesus Christ / have overcome death ..."[24] I have heard dislike of the "you who" phrase offered as the reason for the avoidance of these structures. There is even at least one *you who*, though not in a collect but in a not-much-frequented canticle that begins

> O Lord almighty and God of our forebears
> you who made heaven and earth in all their glory ... .[25]

These seem to be sports; the general principle is that where a relative clause would be in the present or perfect it is disallowed.

"You who" would be used if the second person plural is insisted upon and if the shorter forms like "who have" and "who make" are for some reason rejected. There is, however, no grammatical or stylistic reason why a "contemporary" Agnus Dei should not begin, "O Lamb of God, You who take away the sin of the world ... ." If that is what prayer demands that is what prayer must have. "You who" is in fact commonplace in novels and on stage (I append a short anthology).

One cannot help suspecting that the refusal to use the relative second person plurals except with a past tense is the effect of grammatical as well as stylistic nervousness. The

[24] Fifth Sunday of Easter; when I heard this in church the priest got it wrong and said "has" for "have".
[25] "The Song of Manasseh", GS Misc 594, p. 129.

cheekily entitled Book of Common Prayer for Use in the Church in Wales (1984) may have been a cautionary example. It prints a lot of bad grammar in the collects. I have no information as to whether this was done on purpose to try to acclimatize a new form in modern English, or whether because the compilers just didn't master the grammar. The latter has to be, in view of the chaotic mixture in the book, more probable. The Wales collect for Septuagesima begins, "Almighty God, who has created the heavens and earth, and has made man in thine own image ... " where even the third person is inconsistent, going back to the second person for the possessive "thine". Trinity 20 similarly begins "Almighty God, who shows to those who are in error the light of thy truth .... " The switch to third person is very emphatic on St Stephen's Day, when the collect ends " ... to thee blessed Jesus, who lives and reigns ... " and with a past tense when on Ash Wednesday Cranmer's lovely collect is replaced by "Lord, who for our sake did fast .... " On the other hand the Gloria in Excelsis retains "that takest", Second in Advent has the correct "Blessed Lord, who hast caused all holy Scriptures to be written ... " and Christmas Day begins correctly, "Almighty God, who hast given us .... " Whatever the explanation, they produced a number of collects of the form "O God, who does so and so .... " If any sense is made of the change from the address to God to a third-person verb it can only be that prayer is relinquished in favour of an aside to the congregation, as, "O God, our Heavenly Father, [*aside*] who has brought us together as members of the Army Cadet Force .... "[26] With the "has" this ceases to be a prayer and becomes an announcement. "Our Father who is

[26] Service of Celebration to mark the Silver Jubilee of the Amalgamation of the Hereford & Worcester Army Cadet Forces, Hereford Cathedral, 20 May 2000.

in heaven" is no. 552 in *Mission Praise*, 1990, but that is said to be "Caribbean".

James Hogg has one such ungrammatical form, "Oh, dog of hell, it is you who has done this!"[27] I have never noticed it elsewhere in English Literature. Even some experienced clergy, it is true, get into trouble when extemporizing relative clauses in prayer and tend to go into the third person. "You who receives our prayer," I heard recently. This, presumably, is why the embargo does not apply when the verb in the relative clause is in the past tense, for there the form of the verb is the same for third person singular and all persons plural, so the possibility of ungrammaticality is removed. Only the second singular would demand an inflection. Oddly enough, there seems to be less trouble in church with the second person singular, when the priest may remember that the verb is going to end *-st*. The plural forms are nevertheless quite manageable by any literate person, and illiteracy is not much of an excuse for not using them. The real stylistic objection to them is that we expect the second person singular, "...that takest away..." and so on, as the natural English form.

The "exclusively contemporary" rejection of "thou" does lead to a special modern liturgical style. The address followed by main-clause statement of attribute, "Lamb of God, you take away the sins of the world" and so on, is quite unnatural outside church. The question is whether it can be made natural inside. Here we have something characteristic of the "contemporary". It defines itself, as we have seen, by

[27] *The Private Memoirs and Confessions of a Justified Sinner*, ed. John Carey, Oxford, 1969, repr. 1977, p. 78. Hogg, the self-styled Ettrick Shepherd, is magnificently lettered; he may have committed this solecism deliberately as the appropriately unheroic dying words of a not quite heroic character. For instance Hogg gets the first-person equivalent right: "...to me it signifies nothing, who know too well..." (*Ibid.*, p. 191) as well as the commoner second person singular: "thou who art a worm". (*Ibid.*, p. 101)

difference from the traditional, but we may question whether it succeeds in becoming ordinary and natural. Cranmer's collect form did just that.

The lexis of prayer is always and necessarily special. Where prayer cannot afford any suggestion of oddity or eccentricity is its rhythm. The just-quoted Guidelines say this too: "The language should be rhythmic and flow easily, but take care not to have a repetitive poetic 'dum-de-dum'." Not pausing for the full-dress rebuke called for by the philistine assumption that poetry is repetitive, I observe that in this instance the Guidelines were ignored by the composers of Common Worship. Their prayers again and again do lapse into a repetitive dum-de-dum.

This comment is so simple and elementary that I have asked myself more than once whether I must not be mistaken. I have always contended that the established view of the English versification of the fifteenth century is incredible, because it requires us to believe that Chaucer's friends and disciples forgot how he wrote verse. But I have to observe something even stranger of the prayers of Common Worship. Everything that is not verse, M. Jourdain's maître de philosophie assured him, is prose, and everything that is not prose is verse. The Liturgical Commission and Synod have gone one better than Molière's splendid joke and produced strings of words that are neither prose nor verse. I demonstrated this on the publication of the new collects[28]—"demonstrated" according to the strictest canons of Popperian science, for nobody has refuted me, and to the best of my knowledge nobody has even tried. Until they do, my case counts as established. I am not in doubt about this,

[28] *Faith and Worship* 44, Summer, 1998, pp. 26–32.

and could not be without wondering whether I too have forgotten the difference between verse and prose, I who have spent years on the subject.[29] But since the situation is so extraordinary, I have taken two precautions. Firstly, wherever possible I quote phrases I have heard in church phrased and stressed as I report. Secondly I submitted the case to a group of literary friends, for the most part non-churchgoers, and all lovers of poetry but uninterested in prosody and quite accustomed to telling me I am wrong about the importance I attach to it. They agreed that what I observe of the new collects is simply factual. Literary criticism is normally a matter of opinion, but prosody was always traditionally part of grammar, and there is often no more doubt about a scansion than the clause analysis of a sentence, so I am afraid I don't think what follows is seriously disputable.

Jeremy Bentham's definition of prose (printed to fill the line up to the right hand margin) is true in the sense that if words are printed "as verse" we do read them as such if we can, rather than as prose. The art of writing prose, Aristotle told us, is to make it "numerous" but not metrical. If prose is lineated as verse this is not possible. Pauses are introduced at the ends of lines that are not present between the members of a prose period, and phrases are shaped and stressed wrongly.

Any short group of syllables in English can become part of a verse line in one or more metres. The reader confronted with an English phrase, out of context, of less than eight syllables, cannot know whether it "is" accentual-syllabic verse or prose. In one context it will be the one, in another the other. That's prose, but:

[29] Cf. my books *Chaucer's Prosody*, Cambridge, 1971, and *The Establishment of Modern English Prose*, Cambridge, 1998.

> In *one* context it will be
> The one, as you just now did see:
> Printing it right and without any pother
> Hey presto! makes in another the other.

The metrical readings result from the verse lineation.

Try this as a party game: take any grammatical phrase of seven or eight syllables of English and incorporate them in one or more verse-forms. The one who gets most different verse-forms is the winner. ("*Try* this as a *par*ty game": trochaic, or "Try *this* as a *par*ty-game": amphibracers.)

For this reason, lines of verse can always be found embedded in prose by anyone who cares to look and to phrase and stress accordingly. But unless a writer deliberately aims at verse effects, or is incompetent, the possible verse movements will submit to the varied feet and phrases of prose. Occasionally the hint of verse can be effective in prose, but it is an effect very easily overdone. My own view, though I know others may dissent, is that the death of Jo in *Bleak House* is a wonderful moment, and that ends with a rhetorical flourish of which the last ten syllables are a line of blank verse:

> And dying thus around us every day.

It is far commoner for Dickens to use too much blank verse and weaken his effect. When Victorian novelists want intensity and emotion they take to blank verse, which often sounds mechanical, a contrivance that saves the novelist the trouble of making anything fresh or individual.

Competence in prose writing largely consists in making and joining phrases in ways a reader can easily follow. The Prayer Book shows how rhythmical prose in English can be constructed. The Prayer Book gives the congregation useful assistance with the parts they are to speak by beginning new rhythmic groups with capital letters; similarly Coverdale's psalms are printed in (prose) verses divided by colons into rhythmic groups that classical rhetoric called *cola*.[30] But any suggestion that any of these are new lines of verse is just wrong and confusing.

The first time we read a poem set out in verse lines we identify the metre from the opening line or so. Opening an anthology and coming upon

> Glory to God in the highest,
> and peace to his people on earth,[31]

we would naturally start in the metre of "'Twas Christmas Day in the Workhouse ..." and so congregations habitually do in church. After a stanza break this metre stops and another starts. We seem to be reading *vers libre*, in which the reader will be particularly on the look-out for metrical patterns because they vary line by line. In this example, after a not quite regular trochaic tetrameter, we go on to a quatrain in the metre first found in the deadly verses of the early-Middle-English *Ormulum* and well known in many a ballad and hymn, starting at the second line:

>   almighty God and Father,
> we worship you, we give you thanks,
>   we praise you for your glory. [my indention]

Te tum te tum te tumte / Te tum te tum te tum te tum / Te tum te tum te tumte. If this were prose it would be far less awful, because the jog-trot alternating stress would not be so prominent. But when words are printed as verse we look for verse, and in Common Worship, as in ASB, he that seeketh

[30] For a fuller discussion see the chapter "Cranmer's Commonwealth" in my *Establishment of Modern English Prose*.
[31] Common Worship Order One Gloria in Excelsis, reprinted from ASB.

findeth. The Prayer of Humble Access, prose carefully composed for the single voice of the priest, is now, suitably modernized, recited by congregations. The Rite A version repeated in Common Worship Order One begins

> We do not presume
> to come to this your table, merciful Lord,

which (1) inserts a senseless line-end pause where there is no speech- or prose-pause and (2) reinforces the inappropriate conversion to congregational speaking by turning the first five syllables into an acephalic iambic trimeter: *We* do *not* pre*sume*, as it is normally boomed, after which we go into crudish blank verse that overemphasizes *come* and *this*. A ready and easy way of turning Cranmer's prose into nonsense. By exactly the same method that post-Victorian elegist made so basic a phrase as "dust to dust, ashes to ashes" into nonsense: by forcing us to read it as bad verse.

The practice of printing prose as if it were verse is not, of course, new with Common Worship or even with ASB. It goes far back into the misty origins of the liturgical revolution. The oldest explanation I have found is Bishop Buchanan's:[32] if the Lord's Prayer is set out in short lines the congregation knows when to breathe. The highly educated modern congregation can no longer be trusted to read prose, or to know the Lord's Prayer, and so it is cut up into phrases of a line each. This would, in our days of not worrying about using paper unnecessarily, have the same function as the Prayer Book's initial capitals; unluckily it also turns the prose into verse.

The extreme moment is perhaps the Revised Common Lectionary, in use in many of our churches in a Mowbrays

[32] Cf. above, p. 33.

edition, 1998, which prints *everything* as verse! every lesson of the Bible! even in the New Revised Standard Version which is supposed to descend directly from the Authorized Version. In the service-books the resultant lines are most frequently iambic, often blank verse, but sometimes more rollickingly anapaestic, as

> regard not our sins but the faith of your Church . . . .[33]

te tum te te tum te te tum te te tum.

The collects of Common Worship use very frequently the longer Trinitarian endings usually saved by the Prayer Book for the greater occasions, of which

> Through Jesus Christ your son our Lord

is a very frequent part. Seeing this as a line of verse there is no way for the common reader not to take it as iambic tetrameter, te tum te tum te tum te tum. The new Second in Advent has already confirmed the impression by beginning

> O Lord, raise up, we pray, your power

—which sounds like, and perhaps is, the beginning of a bad hymn in common metre, going woodenly te tum te tum te tum te tum. In case we should miss this the feet are helpfully separated by commas. The new First Sunday of Lent leads up to the tetrameter "through Jesus Christ your son our Lord" with other verses:

> and, as you know our weakness,
> so may we know your power to save;
> through Jesus Christ your son our Lord,
> who is alive and reigns with you.

Iambic trimeter followed by three iambic tetrameters. There is no way of not getting into the metre and reading accord-

[33] ASB, p. 904.

ingly, with bad stress-patterns. The verse is so mechanical that a conscious effort would have to be made not to emphasize its jog-trot regularity. "Who *is* alive" is possible once in a while for emphasis, but when it is heard most Sundays must sink into cliché.

The effects are so frequent and so pronounced that they must have been intentional, even if not fully conscious. Of the new eucharistic prayers in Order One the most thoroughly versified is the Evangelical-inclined D:

> Almighty God, good Father to us all,
> your face is turned towards your world. [not the wall?]
> In love you gave us Jesus your son
> to rescue us from sin and death.
> Your word goes out to call us home
>   to the city where angels sing your praise.
> We join with them in heaven's song.

After the opening line of blank verse it settles down to iambic tetrameters to which, despite the hypermetrical syllables in "Jesus" and "city", contemporary poetry editors would probably object that they are too regular. This is not a one-off effect. The prayer keeps it up!

> The crowds came out to see your Son,
>   yet at the end they turned on him.[34]
> On the night he was betrayed
> he came to table with his friends
>   to celebrate the freedom of your people.

Back to blank verse at the end, but the line before is poetic diction for the sake of the verse. Prose would surely have had something more like "He sat down to dine". This Evangelical-flavoured prayer naturally goes on to quote a hymn that some of us sang at Sunday school. After the last-

[34] The indention is puzzling and misleading because it makes us expect a rhyme.

quoted line the President (as he/she still is in Common Worship) has a paragraph break then ends:

This is his story.
All **This is our song**

but it still isn't straightforward verse, because instead of continuing as they must expect, and perhaps bursting into singing for it, "Praising the saviour all the day long" they have "**Hosanna in the highest**", which doesn't scan. The phrase is repeated with the original with "our story" for "his story" twice later in the prayer. There is no way of not taking these lines as verse, but equally there is no way of knowing what to do with them as verse or how to accommodate them to the following prose.

Prayer G (the one that will give any not-half-asleep congregation pause for thought with its puzzling category of an *echo of silent music*) has the brisk Longellow-like narrative

On the night before he died
he came to supper with his friends
and, taking bread, he gave you thanks.

This may wel be rym doggerel, quod he or in more modern idiom blank doggerel. The effect of versification is to drain the already flat prose (if it was drafted in prose) into complete insignificance.

In like manner, the verse of the prayer provided for *after a suicide* cannot have been an accident:

God our strength and our redeemer [trochaic tetrameter as Hiawatha]
you do not leave us in this life [iambic tetrameter]
nor abandon us in death. [*ditto* acephalic]
Hear our prayer for those in despair [four-beat with internal rhyme]

> when days are full of darkness ["Now the day is over"]
> and the future empty of hope["Night is drawing nigh"]
> Renew in them your sustaining strength [four-beat; internal assonance]
> for we believe that there is nothing[iambic tetrameter]

—and there you get the resultant unevadable nonsense, for the iambic metre end-stops the line and makes "nothing" a declaration of belief.[35]

The collect for the so-called Fourth Sunday before Lent starts

> O God,
> you know us to be set . . . .

How can anyone not take this as an end-stopped iambic trimeter, necessarily suggesting jelly? If printed as prose it would be much better phrased: "O God, you know us to be set in the midst of so many and great dangers . . . ." The forcing into verse does the damage.

Most of the new Sunday collects are based on traditional ones. The Commission's chance of quite new creation came with the much-extended "lesser festivals". George Herbert day is 27 February. The collect begins

> King of glory, king of peace,

which most likely the congregation will just have sung as the opening line of Herbert's famous hymn. How on earth are we meant not to read it as the same verse line in the collect? But then we go on to a not-quite limerick line, "who called your servant George Herbert" (it only needs "to" after "called" to be perfect limerick). Bishop Ken is likewise commemorated in a collect beginning with a line minimally

[35] Cf. a form of *confessing the good* retained from ASB, "I confess to you . . . the good I have left undone . . . ." (GS120A, n.d., p. 19)

altered from his most famous hymn, "O God, from whom all blessings flow". And so on.

But then again, the verse is not consistent. It mixes with prose, for instance again and again in the doxologies. Third Sunday of Epiphany begins with the frequent horribly regular iambic tetrameters:

> through Jesus Christ your Son our Lord
> who is alive and reigns with you ...

so that when at last we get to a genuine bit of prose, "in the unity of the Holy Spirit, / one God, now and for ever" we don't know what to do.

To add to the confusion parts of Common Worship apparently meant to be prose are printed unjustified, i.e. with lines of different length; and the versified prose of the collects, canticles and absolutions does not use a capital letter for the beginnings of lines in the usual way; so it is sometimes tricky to know whether verse or prose is intended.

I do not believe that the Liturgical Commission were deliberately mixing verse and prose, like the medieval form called "cadence" with which Chaucer begins the tale of Melibee. There are hints of cadence in the Prayer Book, for instance in the incorporation of verse lines into the Prayer of Humble Access ("Grant us therefore, gracious Lord", trochaic, and the complete hexameter "and our souls washed through his most precious blood"). But for the unrhetorical modern age "cadence" is an unlikely explanation.

When the "considerable body of new prayer material" was in draft and I mentioned the prose-as-verse to Canon Perham, as he then was, he replied off the cuff with the old explanation that the practice helps the congregation with phrasing.[36] I did not find out how, and I will not speculate about what we are meant to do with the sub-verses, slightly indented, which ASB and Common Worship frequently use. In any case, in Common Worship the prose-as-verse is used for the collects, to be read by the celebrant, where no question of congregational speaking arises.

Common as the practice of setting out material in verse lines has become in the new liturgies, "no precedent will justify absurdity", especially not the precedent of ASB in the act of being reformed. Common Worship, which should have taken the chance of restoring decent ordinary prose, has in fact driven the prose-as-verse much further than ASB.

There are only two possible explanations of the half-verse of these collects. Either these composers of liturgy and all the revisers failed to notice the ludicrous effects of their prose-as-verse. Or they did it on purpose. These are almost equally hard to credit, but after considerable puzzling I incline to the second.

What seems to have happened over the years is that, nobody having got across to the liturgists that they need to know whether they are writing prose or verse, the dim realization that prose has been half turned into verse by lineation led to verse-like declamations in church which in turn became a manner, then a conscious style in which *vers libre* is groped for. This then became the stand-in for the "liturgical language that is poetic, rhythmic, resonant and memorable" which Dean Perham wanted.

This history does not solve the puzzles. How can it have happened that a literate and meticulously supervised group

[36] I followed this up with a two-page memo making the elementary point about verse, so I now state the objections in public with a very clear conscience.

can have printed the line

> Hear our prayer for those in despair

without noticing anything wrong with it?—the comic effect made in just the same way as in that couplet on Queen Victoria, by the unlucky creation of rhyming verse. Why, with all the committees, revisions, re-revisions, all the processes that go into approval by Synod... did nobody notice how frequently silly the results are? Have they no access *at all* to the ordinary common language and common judgement?

I think the answer, though hardly less puzzling than the question, can only be that the contemporary church has got used to the style, as the modern style, at the same time as becoming increasingly insulated from the ordinary world. If "hear our prayer for those in despair" was intended to take us out into the highways and byeways and tempt people in by speaking to them in their own tongues it has in fact had the opposite effect of making something only churchy.

But though not contemporary or colloquial this style is modern and even characteristic of the age. No previous generation would have created nonentity in quite this way. It's not prose, not verse, almost not-language, if we still expect language to make sense. In Jane Austen's day the clergy were wisely kept from tampering with the Prayer Book. If her Mr Collins had written collects they would have been like these.

Some of the advice about prayers quoted above is better reversed:

> Use sentences of ordinary length and complexity.
>
> Remember you are talking to God and do not think it necessary to talk down to One whose intelligence is greater than ours, or to suppose that He does not

understand standard English.
Address God as "Thou".
If you have not the gift of praying in public without making people giggle, refrain.

At one point, though, I am at one with the Liturgical Commission. The quoted "guidelines" are for occasional "material", one-off intercessions and the like, not for Common Worship. I regret that I have nevertheless heartily to recommend the application of the last recommendation to the whole set of Common Worship collects: "Be prepared to throw it away after using it, and to do it differently next time." I would recommend one improvement even on this. Throw it away now, without using it at all, and don't spend a lot of parish money obtaining copies.

Let me repeat my expression of relief that the Prayer Book is given a place in Common Worship. But ... we are told by flyers of the Liturgical Publishing Group, chaired by the Bishop of Guildford, that the 1662 Eucharist, Morning and Evening Prayer as reprinted in Common Worship are "set out in a modern style to match the rest of the new book." This sounds good: let us by all means have the best typography we can.[37] What is meant, however, by "modern" is principally verse lineation and paragraphing by line-space not indention. The latter is modern in offices and company reports. Neither is used for ordinary prose in books or newspapers. *The Sun*, I regret, is modern and contemporary, but prints prose full out to the right hand margin as Bentham says, and does not leave line-spaces. So, regrettably, the inclusion of the Book of Common Prayer in Common

[37] Though on the one hand the "new" (and admirable) practice of printing rubrics in red is a pleonasm, and on the other it is very questionable whether the use of a sans serif font in a book this size is either modern or sensible.

Worship is not a straightforward recognition of the centrality of Cranmer, for this is the Book of Common Prayer half-versified.

In the Prayer of Humble Access, as I observed, one trochaic tetrameter and one hexameter are subsumed into the prose, but it remains prose, however rhythmically crafted. The regularly repeating feet lift a passage which begins in deliberately low style (to follow the medieval categories), with runs largely of monosyllables like "so much as to gather up the crumbs" evidently intended for a single voice not over-loud. The effect is spoiled if the passage is treated as verse, as it now is; the hexameter is far too prominent, and the compilers have found another iambic pentameter I had never noticed, and which does not occur in the modernized version of Order One,[38]

> whose property is always to have mercy.

As verse, to be frank, it isn't good. Cranmer couldn't write decent verse when he tried, so what is to be expected when verse is force upon his prose? Look at this edition to find out, on every page.

The great consecration prayer, on the other hand, is left as prose, but fragmented into modern office-style paragraphs with no indention and separated by spaces; it is also much interrupted by rubrics, so that any help the typography might give with realizing the wonderful unity of the two sentences is dissipated.

The [new] Collects in Traditional Language depart from actual traditional language in the same basic and elementary way.[39] The already quoted Ash Wednesday collect repro-

[38] The precedent was in fact set by the Church in Wales book.

[39] As well as in minor ways. "World without end" is not permitted, for instance, though it is a much closer translation of the Greek originals than "now and for ever".

duces the words of the Book of Common Prayer down as far as the new pompous doxology, but it prints them as verse, making a third line that is a fourteener:

> and dost forgive the sins of all them that are penitent

Fourteeners are just about the most thumping English metre, fortunately disused since about 1570 until revived for the "modern, colloquial" Prayer D of Order One with lines such as

> he touched untouchables with love and washed the guilty clean

and

> and is alive with you to plead for us and all the world.

Nobody would find a fourteener in the prose of the Prayer of Humble Access; as verse there is no alternative.

The failure of style under discussion being so elementary, it is not uncalled for to restate a truism of literary criticism, that in language sound *is* sense: get the rhythm [40] wrong and the sense must be wrong. Anybody who doesn't realize that prose rhythm is not verse rhythm, but that both are at the heart of the meaning of language, should leave liturgy well alone.

What I see, then, in the "may" of absolutions and blessings, the refusal of second-person relative clauses, in the funk about the second person singular, in the incompetent rhythmic writing, together with the continued use of bits of

[40] I have discussed rhythm in a larger sense, how parts join together to make wholes, in *Prayers for the New Babel*, chapters 4 and 5. Everything I said applies equally to Order One. Printed with that Order is a page of "Order One *Structure*". It is effectively a contents page, but what is supposed to make the parts coalesce is unclear.

the essential English lexis of prayer, really is an exclusively contemporary language of prayer, but only in the sense of being the ordinary one mutilated. There ought to be a society for the prevention of cruelty to English.

If this large collection of "prayer material" was composed deliberately and did not run into serious stylistic objections, that says something very alarming about the present state of the collective mind of the Church of England.[41] Once, the bishops of the established church were expected to be learned men. Following that, they were expected to be at least competent writers of English prose. Publishers nowadays collect "endorsements" (others associate them with breaking the law on the road) from the influential to try to get their books sold. *The Christian Year*, the first publication of the Common Worship collects, included this one from the Bishop of Guildford on behalf of the Liturgical Commission:

> This is an exciting moment. In publishing *Calendar, Lectionary and Collects* we are offering the Church the first step in a new generation of worship material. This will be both widely welcomed and used in the parishes, help us to deepen our life of prayer and hear the word of God.

I wonder whether any copies were sold as a result. Is the third quoted sentence grammatical without an *and* after the comma to pick up the *both* or, if the *and* before the comma is the one, what is the syntactic status of the rest of the sentence? Does anybody believe for a moment that anyone is excited? by "worship material"? Can there be a step in a new generation? If the metaphors are not just a mixture of corpses, is not the first step in generation sexual intercourse?

[41] Cf. "Those who seek to know the mind of the Church of England in the last quarter of the twentieth century will find it in this book . . . ." (ASB Preface, p. 10)

How did anything so incompetent come to be written by a bishop then used by SPCK in its promotion material? The liturgical specialists of the Established Church, duly approved and authorized, are now not competently in command of written English.

Liturgy was originally, in Greek, a public work, sometimes onerously at the expense of private individuals. In the Septuagint the word stretches as far as the work done to get King David back over Jordan after the rebellion of Absalom, so what there goes into the Greek as liturgy comes into English as "a ferry boat".[42] I like the idea of the liturgy as something made to conduct us, as Cranmer put it, "unto the throne of the heavenly grace". The basic question as with all useful things is whether it works. "Into the tomb the great Queen dashes" doesn't work as elegy. I do have to make the same judgement about many of the new collects. They don't work, and for the same reason, they are just too badly composed.

Dean Perham re-uses an unsound defence of the Commissioners' rhetoric. He wants to "introduce" (should it not have been "reintroduce"?) "liturgical language that is poetic, rhythmic, resonant and memorable". But unluckily "the creation of a new liturgical rhetoric, which cannot be contrived and has to emerge naturally, probably through the trial and error of the wordsmiths, is a slow business."[43] Oh no it isn't; nor does a smith of any kind work by trial and error, nor would he get paid if he did or if he asked clients to wait indefinitely for the work to be done properly, nor is it reasonable to ask congregations to suffer self-confessedly unsuccessful work generation after generation. What has

[42] 2 Samuel xix.18.
[43] *Celebrate the Christian Story*, 1997, p. 5.

been emerging naturally is the half-baked verse we have looked at.

In much the same way the Alternative Service Book 1980 recommended us to "recognize their [words'] transience and imperfection; to treat them as a ladder, not a goal . . . ."[44] By all means think of words as a ladder, like Jacob's, with the angels ascending and descending. But the next time you prune the pear tree do not trust yourself to a ladder self-confessedly transient and imperfect. The question about the ladder is whether it will let you down. Similarly the question is whether what the same paragraph calls the "faltering words of men" will *work*. Writing liturgical prose is a job of work which should come easily in a church with such a distinguished tradition of it, and in fact good liturgical prose was written in the twentieth century. There was no serious stylistic problem with the 1928 proposed revision of the Prayer Book, nor with Series One. Did the members of the Liturgical Commission hear the decommissioning service for the royal yacht *Britannia*? The congregation of ordinary sailors as well as dignitaries heard well-composed new prayers—in prose—alongside the old ones still in use in the Navy. (Perhaps Her Majesty the Queen should be appointed Chairperson of the Liturgical Commission.) But good liturgical prose will not be written if its mainspring is difference from the Prayer Book.

Prayer Book prose cannot be precisely dated because nobody is quite sure when Cranmer began work in earnest, but from the evidence of his letters it took him about five years to develop from the wandering Latinate stuff that English prose then was. He had no time to allow good prose to emerge naturally, which is in any case not a practical

[44] Preface, p. 11.

method. Cranmer did the work on language because without it he could not make common prayer. If there is a genuine need in language, ways will be found, and perhaps that is what is meant by poetic genius. But the notion that we must wait for the next millennium (or possibly the one after?) for good new liturgical writing manages to be simultaneously defeatist and arrogant, for it did not occur to Bishop Stancliffe's commission any more than Dean Jasper's simply to recognize that they could not do their work. There would have been no disgrace in that, but such is not the nature of modern bureaucracy. Here, I think, we see something genuinely contemporary and not confined to the Church: a clerisy (to use Coleridge's term) unable to discharge its responsibilities but without any intention of giving up any of its power. The result in this case is that those congregations of the Church of England who reject the Book of Common Prayer or use it in the newly versified form are stuck indefinitely with English not competently written.

One hopes for peace within the established church; and let me repeat that the effort to bring back the Book of Common Prayer into the mainstream is very welcome, even in its versified form. Honesty is still the best charity: we do as we would be done by. Common Worship is certainly different from the Alternative Service Book 1980, adding to the flatness of the latter the "poetic, rhythmic, resonant and memorable" new versified pomposities. Both styles, I regret I have to say are, in their different ways, stupid.

The "contemporary" style is a misnomer: the real alternatives are the ordinary religious style of the language, and the same style smudged and dumbed.

I draw a practical moral, particularly for Prayer Book churches. We must all have had experience of the priests who use the Prayer Book for the office but then pray extempore using second plural forms. Why they do this I am not sure. There may be the unfortunate hint that we are now approaching closer to God by becoming less formal. (Actually t'other way round: "Thou" is bound to be intimate though not, perhaps, familiar.) It is true that in Shakespeare singular and plural can alternate in the same scene in ways it is hard to give reasons for. But now, when in standard English the second person singular is normal only in prayer, I don't think it mixes well with the plural. This mixture is at best messy. If we are using a form of service with the ordinary second singular of prayer, like the ordinary form of the Lord's Prayer, why drag in the plural? I think we should stick to the second person singular. "Thou" belongs to the language of prayer as naturally as "O" and "grant" and "amen".

"Contemporary" language must never use the second person singular. Yet the Lord's Prayer, if it is generally known at all, is generally known in its "traditional" version, complete with copious use of the second person singular possessives. When a newspaper wants to quote or make up a commandment you can bet it will use the "Thou shalt" form.[45] When God addresses a commandment to Homer Simpson it begins "Thou shalt". "Thou" is as contemporary as "O".

Somebody ought to carry out some research: my prediction is that many, many people would realize that when the second person singular is used, as when "O" or "Amen" are

[45] First leader in *Financial Times* 18 March 2000, "Thou shalt not raise taxes." The same broadsheet can appeal to the Te Deum: "Fellowship of Prophets" was the name of the Lex Column, 6 June 2000, used to refer to the Bank for International Settlements.

said, we are praying—more than would be able to attach any meaning whatever to "the mediator of the new covenant"[46] or to "the old leaven of corruption and wickedness"[47] and such necessary phrases which need much more by way of explanation—or to "Our love for you is like a morning cloud",[48] which, in the absence of a scriptural context, anybody would with the best will in the world have difficulty in understanding.

Appendix

"You Who", A brief anthology

And happy you who, by propitious fate
On great Apollo's sacred standard wait. (Roscommon,
"An Essay on Translated Verse", 3–4)

"If there were sic a day of trial put to you, Reuben, you, who are a young lad . . . ." (Scott, *The Heart of Midlothian*, ed. Tony Inglis, 1994, p. 439)

"I would fain say something, not so much concerning the Chinese and Sandwich Islanders as you who read these pages, who are said to live in New England . . . ." (Thoreau, *Walden,* Everyman edn, n. d., p. 2)

"Well, I thought it was not like you to do it; you who have such good principles of your own." (Susan Ferrier, *Destiny*, New Edn, n. d. [Routledge], p. 92)

"To you, who have so lately been seeing so many fine pictures in Italy . . . ." (*Ibid.*, p. 149)

[46] GS Misc 594, p. 76.
[47] GS 1280A, p. 41.
[48] *Ibid.*, p. 15.

"… how will he bear your absence—you who are now every thing to him?" (*Ibid.*, p. 151)

"This is to impress you—who are a young friend of the family—with a due sense of the excellence of the garden … ." (Dickens, *Sketches by Boz*, n. d. [Hazell, Watson & Viney], p. 72)

"… we know that if it were you who happened to wake him … ." (Fanny Trollope, *The Vicar of Wrexhill*, 1837, repr. Bristol, 1996, p. 10)

"… you, who are young … ." (Margaret [*sic*; British Library Cataloguing *Mrs*] Oliphant, *The Curate in Charge*, 1875; repr., Gloucester, 1985, p. 194)

"'It is you who are mistaken,' said the young rector." (*Ibid.*, p. 202)

"And you who write so perfectly!" (George Eliot, *Daniel Deronda*, Cabinet Edn, n. d., I, p. 172)

"It is you who will decide … ." (*Ibid.*, III, p. 28)

"You who put up with my singing of Schubert … ." (*Ibid.*, II, p. 242)

"It is you who have given shape … ." (*Ibid.*, III, p. 315)

"…you whose life has been given up to the service of God —you who have put His service far above all earthly affections; you who have shown yourself so strong … ." (M. E. Braddon, *The Fatal Three*, 1888, repr. Stroud, 1997, p. 155)

"… you who have said so many bitter things of the fools who fall in love, and the still greater fools who marry, *you* who stand alone … !" (*Ibid.*, p. 186)

"It is you who have made me see myself clearly." (Leo Tolstoy, *Father Sergius and Other Stories and Plays*, ed. Hagberd Wright, 1911, p. 41)

"'Never mind, it is you who must pardon me,' she said … ." (*Ibid.*, p. 65)

"And you, who have told me a hundred times. . . ." (C. S. Lewis, *The Silver Chair*, n. d., p. 137)

"It seems to be you, who really have to be separated." (I. Compton-Burnett, *More Women than Men*, repr. 1960, p. 60)

"It's you who are playing the tricks, Charles." (Noël Coward, *Blithe Spirit*, somewhere)

"And it is you who are responsible for all this. It was you who in the first place allowed the Athenians to fortify their city. . . ." (Thucydides, *History of the Peloponnesian War*, transl. Rex Warner, 1954, repr. 1956, p. 49)

"As for me, I am the same as I was, and do not alter; it is you who have changed." (Pericles as reported by Thucydides, *Ibid.*, p. 130)

"And do you know why, you who so innocently keep his company, you who imprudently invite him into your houses. . . ? For it is *he* who has the plague, *he* who unknowing harbours it inside him. . . ." (Nicholas Somers, "The Muse of Difficulty", *The Human World*, 13, 1974, pp. 32–33)

". . . you who are master of your own destiny. . ." (Martin Crimp, unpublished translation of Marivaux, *The Triumph of Love,* Almeida Theatre, 1999)

". . . you who process all things in cosmic order. . ." (David Stuttard, unpublished translation of Aeschylus, *Agamemnon*, Actors of Dionysus Production, 1999)

". . . you who bring all things to fulfilment. . ." (*Ibid.*)

Variant: rhyme interrupted

"Then it's you, is it, sir, who have encouraged and brought about this match?" (*The Pickwick Papers,* chapter xlviii)

" 'And it is you—darling—who have given me that happiness,' he said, smiling shyly." (*Father Sergius*, *ed.cit.*, p. 41)

"... my real need was for you, my God, who are the food of the soul ... ." (St Augustine, *Confessions*, transl. R. S. Pine-Coffin, 1961, repr. n. d., p. 55)

Other persons appear fluently, as

"... especially to me who have been often apt to amuse myself with Visions ..." (Swift, *Gulliver's Travels*, ed. John Hayward, III. x)

"... me who am ..." (R. L. Stevenson, *Catriona*, 1893, page ref. as Carlyle sometimes says "somewhere adrift in my papers".)

"I beg you will have the goodness to attribute that to me, who have detained her ... .", (Dickens, *Bleak House*, Chapter XIV, "Deportment")

"Yes, Duncan, it is faith in Him who is the Way ..." (*Destiny*, *ed. cit.*, p. 265)

"... confronting poor me, who am so eager to lap it all ..." (*More Women than Men*, *ed. cit.*, p. 74)

Though Henry James is at home with "you who" ("Yes, it's you who have destroyed him ... ." ("The Papers", *The Better Sort*, 1903, p. 269) he sometimes prefers the variant "you that", reminiscent of the "them that" also eschewed, on obscure grounds, by the Liturgical Commission: "'It's you that are morbid,' she answered." (*Ibid.*, p. 255) "It's *you* that are ... ." (*Ibid.*, p. 301) James, naturally, is not alone with "you that ... ": "Don't talk of not having spirits, you that are all life!" (Maria Edgeworth, *Belinda*, 1801, repr. 1896, p. 15) "... you that I thought would receive my last breath ... ." (*Ibid.*, p. 29) "You see a long way into my heart, you that are the core of it." (D. K. Broster, *The Flight of the Heron*, 1925, repr. 1951, p. 21)

To the very limited extent that newspapers can be taken as an index of idiom, "that" for "who" is still idiomatic:

"True, there are some, such as the British manufacturers that are struggling with the sterling impact of the euro's downward overshoot, that have a legitimate ground for complaint." (*The Financial Times* first leader 6 May 2000)

"You that" seems to be the Liturgical Commission's centuries-old escape route from "you who" if they desire contemporary colloquiality.

VIII
The Theology of Common Worship

Peter Mullen

> The Book of Common Prayer (1662) is authorised permanently and is completely untouched by this revision process.[1]

Let us look first at Common Worship's Baptism, Marriage and Funeral Services, because these are the Services used by the occasional churchgoers who represent the largely unchurched general public. In the Prayer Book, The Public Baptism of Infants is a rite which takes sin and the devil seriously. But here it has been re-titled Initiation Services and a rationale is provided for why we require this Service: "This is a demanding task for which you will need the help and grace of God." But don't we need the help and grace of God for everything we do? Some of the new injunctions in Initiation Services are phrased in a style which we are not accustomed to hear in church: "God invites you on a life-long journey..." and "Christian formation must allow an individual's story to be heard." This is not really theological language. It has about it the intonation of the counselling

[1] *Planning for Change*, above, p. 51.

clinic and even something of what has become known as "New Age".

In successful prose or poetry, language and thought are continuous, and the words chosen offer us an immediate presentation of some aspect of reality. But the Introduction to Initiation Services is written in words that obscure meaning:

> It is important to come to these Services with a fresh mind, trying to put aside the approaches which have conditioned thinking while the ASB has been in use. The authorised text needs to be seen not as intrusive legal regulation but as a guide to performance.

But, "Come to these Services with a fresh mind" unavoidably carries the connotation, "Try to forget everything you've ever learnt." The revisers seem to want churchgoers to put aside all recollections of earlier liturgies—the Prayer Book certainly, but also the ASB. Unfortunately, it is not possible to make up liturgical language without leaning heavily on what has been used in the past: in any Christian liturgy such words as "God", "Jesus Christ", "redemption", "forgiveness" are bound to put in an appearance. Indeed, it might be thought that continuity with the past is part of what we mean by "Christian tradition". And the church's theology declares that worshippers here on earth are part of the whole church, here and in heaven; part of a living movement that has a past, present and future. Moreover, as T. S. Eliot said,

> the communication
> Of the dead is tongued with fire beyond the language
> of the living.

A liturgy which takes deliberate account of earlier forms is bound to be richer than one which tries to make all things new—precisely because it contains layers of meaning and resonances which have formed and reflected the experience of Christian centuries past. Historical periods have their particular *character* of course but, though ages come and go, it is basic to Christian belief that the human condition and psychology—"the soul of man"—does not much alter with the passing years. We need to give praise and thanks and to confess our sins just as much as Cranmer's generation and even as the recently vanished ASB generation. There must therefore be continuity and similarity of expression. In fairness, the authors of Common Worship realise this, and many of the prayers and sentences used are much like (or even the same as) what has gone before. Interestingly, this suggests the question why there was thought to be the need for a replacement. I am in a sense stating the obvious truth that it is the character of the doctrine that determines which words shall be used; and since Christian doctrine remains the same in its essentials, then we should not expect too much novelty in the words chosen for its expression.

Again, "Conditioned thinking" is unavoidable. *All* thought is conditioned, for the very good reason that language does not consist entirely of neologisms. Indeed, unconditioned thinking is a contradiction in terms because thinking has to be intentional, actually about something: and what it is about are, so to speak, its conditions. And if we belong to a Christian tradition, we shall inevitably think the same thoughts that our forefathers thought. Therefore, we shall be likely to employ similar words.

The expression "legal regulation" is used pejoratively and we are told it will be seen as "intrusive". This seems to me to be an extremely libertarian, antinomian point of view. There is another and more favourable theological view of the phrase which knows that laws exist not unnecessarily to cramp our style, but for our protection and guidance. The unruly wills and affections of sinners require ordering.

Successful liturgical language effects an immediate presentation of the spiritual mystery. Liturgical language is less successful when it is overwhelmingly discursive and tries to explain the mystery. But attempts to explain what is inexplicable—because transcendent—are bound to result in bathos.

The Prayer Book service The Public Baptism of Infants says, "... by the Baptism of thy well-beloved Son Jesus Christ, in the river Jordan, [Thou] didst sanctify water to the mystical washing away of sin ... ."

Common Worship says, "Now sanctify this water that, by the power of your Holy Spirit, they may be cleansed from sin and born again ... ." Even if we ignore that peremptory "Now", the sensation is of a peculiar flatness of tone in which the priest does not by image and rhythm *evoke* a mysterious spiritual landscape but merely *describes* what (he hopes) is going on. Holy Baptism is a full and holy cure of the most dread disease, and this disease is sin. It is dreadful because, as Scripture tells us, its wages are death. The Prayer Book makes this terrifyingly clear right at the start: "Dearly beloved, forasmuch as all men are conceived and born in sin ... ." Common Worship does not get round to a mention of sin until the candidate makes his "Decision". In fact, the Pelagian tendency permeates this new book. It is as if we must not be led to think badly of ourselves. Modern liturgists have frequently explained to me why they have omitted the words "conceived and born in sin": "We mustn't use language that suggests there is something unclean about sexual intercourse or giving birth—language that is also offensive to women." But the Prayer Book neither implies physical uncleanness, nor disparages women: the sin it refers to is Original Sin which, according to such primitive minds as the author of Genesis, St Paul, St Augustine and St Thomas Aquinas, is the heritage and mark of "all men". Common Worship Initiation Services are theologically feeble because they contain no suggestion of this deep sore with which we are all marked. So we are left wondering about the purpose of Holy Baptism. Of course it is a "family occasion" when we publicly welcome a new member of the human race, but there is more to it than that. We receive her into the fellowship of Christ's flock which is the company of those he has redeemed from the severe stain of sin; and in this company the infant will have to learn that there is a fight on, against sin, the world and the devil. To play down the sheer evilness of evil and its spoiling presence in the human heart is at the same time to play down the redeeming work of Christ. I cannot believe that that was part of the Liturgical Commission's intentions.

The revisers also show a disquieting unfamiliarity with the nature of traditional liturgical language. In *The Commentary by the Liturgical Commission on Initiation Services* there is a section entitled "Accessible Language" which says, "The full and rich biblical imagery surrounding baptism and the comparative ignorance of this imagery in many sections of modern society pose a major problem in the drafting of services of Christian initiation." This is certainly true, but their solution to this problem for evangelism is to abandon the full and rich imagery; whereas a better solution would be to present the full and rich imagery so that "sections" of "modern society" might hear it and become enriched by it. People have to be taught. But instead the removal of the fullness and the richness results in their deprivation—and that cannot have been the intention of the Commission either. They claim that the traditional biblical imagery is expressed in "esoteric language". But is it? The Prayer Book's presentation of this imagery is immediate, powerful and memorable. It contains a wonderful evocation of spiritual landscape and the personal involvement of heroes of the faith: "Noah and his family in the ark … the children of Israel through the Red Sea … the baptism of thy well-beloved Son, Jesus Christ in the river Jordan." This is no less than a recitation of our sacred history which is entirely appropriate when a welcome is being made—because it encourages a thrilling sense of belonging, of being part of the greatest story ever told. This is not a question of mere "style" but the reflection of incarnational theology, as we see that the purposes of God are bound up with particular people and places.

A curious rite called "Emergency Baptism" is carried over in an expanded form from ASB into Common Worship. The rubric governing its use makes for interesting reading. It says, "Parents are responsible for requesting emergency baptism for an infant. They should be assured that questions of ultimate salvation or of the provision of a Christian funeral do not depend on whether a child has been baptised." In other words, when is an emergency not an emergency? When it's an emergency baptism! Finally, there is a new prayer called Thanksgiving for Holy Baptism which begins with what appears to be an altogether more mundane sort of emergency: "I saw water flowing from the threshold of the temple." I fear this will provoke wits in the congregation to respond, "Call the Ecclesiastical Insurance Company!"

The three most serious events in life are birth, sex and death. The authors of the Prayer Book knew this and so they produced rites of passage capable of bearing the weight of these occasions. These rites see men and women as, by grace, capable of virtue certainly, but as fundamentally flawed and so always likely go wrong. The old word for this going wrong is "sin". Specific dangers attend every phase of human existence. What plagues men and women for much of our lives is sexual desire; and we all know that unbridled sexual desire causes havoc. That is why the Prayer Book includes all those stern and psychologically accurate words in the Introduction to The Solemnisation of Matrimony in which the couple (and indeed the whole congregation) are admonished concerning: "carnal lusts and appetites ... a remedy against sin, and to avoid fornication; that such persons as have not the gift of continency might marry and so keep themselves undefiled members of Christ's body." As in The Public Baptism of Infants, the Prayer Book is in deadly earnest when it comes to describing the human condition and the deep flaw in our nature by which we are "let and hindered". Therefore matrimony is called "holy". It is not an ornament, but a sacrament. As such it is necessary if we are to be saved from our sinful tendencies and the death which is their consequence. To be sure, it is a stark and urgent message but it is Christian truth.

Compared with this, Common Worship's Marriage Service is unrealistic and shares with the Hollywood musical elements of fantasy. There is no mention of carnal lusts and appetites or of the moral and personal dangers which these things involve. Instead, the bridegroom and the bride have to say to each other, "All that I am I give to you" (retained from ASB). But do they give each other their bad temper and their indigestion? It is like the title of a song by Bing Crosby. If we believe that the marriage ceremony exists in order to bestow, through the sacrament, some help and protection—some remedy against sin—then to leave out all mention of sin is to leave the couple unprotected. Later on the priest may pray (Appendix 7, "Additional Prayers and Collects"), "In gentleness let them be tender with each other's dreams."[2] This is another example of the vague, untheological, touchy-feely language that has displaced such things as, "I require and charge you both as ye will answer at the dreadful day of judgement . . . ." There is no judgement here only sentimental self-indulgence. It is hard to attach a clear meaning to "Let them be tender with each other's dreams." Does it mean, "Don't let them disillusion each other"? But the marriage ceremony is meant to be an example of illusions being swept away at the very beginning of the couple's shared life together. The Solemnisation of Matrimony does just that: it lets the couple know that they are always in the presence of many and great dangers arising out of their own corrupt desires. Moreover it insists that one of the main causes for which matrimony was ordained is the procreation of children. Of course we know that children may be procreated outside marriage but, says the Prayer Book, it is marriage which confers their legitimacy. Common Worship is vague at this point. It says, "It is given as the foundation of family life in which children are [born and] nurtured"—almost as if there were something not providential but accidental about this birth and nurturing.

Common Worship's Marriage Service is a disservice to the couple because it does not prepare them for the reality of what is going to happen to them. Because it leaves out all

[2] GS 1298F, May, 1999, p. 33.

those accurate descriptions of human sexuality and instead offers a psychological world like that in a romantic novel, it is a theological failure. As in Initiation Services the true nature of human personality is obscured by a welter of euphemisms which misrepresent the truth about human character. Again the participants are encouraged to think well of themselves: an art at which, one might reasonably conclude, every man is already his own expert. This evasiveness and Pelagian disregard for human character runs all through Common Worship. Again I have made these points to members of the Liturgical Commission and been told repeatedly, "We have gained fresh insights into human sexuality since Cranmer's time. The Prayer Book was very negative about sex." What fresh insights are these? Has the human species, through copious modern educational projects, outgrown lust and adultery? If so, why are there more single parents than ever, and (according to the government's own figures) ten times as many rapes as fifty years ago as well as 180,000 abortions every year; while two out of every five marriages end in divorce? Still we hear the Pelagian cry, "Nothing to acknowledge; nothing to bewail." The Prayer Book is not "negative" about sex. In fact it is extremely earthy. But it is certainly negative about unlawful sex. In the face of this Marriage Service it is hard to avoid the conclusion that the Liturgical Commission has some sort of problem with traditional Christian moral teaching. Have the words of Freud, Dr Kinsey and Dr Alex Comfort surpassed those of Our Lord Jesus Christ and the apostle Paul? Members of the Liturgical Commission are justly proud of their notions of social gospel and of a version of Christianity which is helpful to society at large. They say, "Marriage enriches society and strengthens community." But do they imagine that the good of society as a whole is furthered by the invention of a rite which fails to take account of fundamental human character? Common Worship's Baptism and Marriage rites do nothing to help a society which has lost its moral landmarks. Well, it is the Prayer Book Commination Service which warns us: "Cursed is he that removeth his neighbour's landmark." Unfortunately, landmark removal has been the trademark of much liturgical revision over these last thirty years.

We see in The Marriage Service the same unstable mixture of sentimentality and tedious bureaucratic language that we found in Initiation Services. The priest introduces the ceremony praying, "... that with delight and tenderness they may know each other in love." But the smoky romantic atmosphere conjured by this vague aspiration sounds odd alongside the Council Tax Office style injunction to the bride and groom, "I am required to ask." The Prayer Book at this point has, "I require and charge you both" which leaves the couple in no doubt that marriage is a holy estate and in deadly seriousness. The weak statement "I am required to ask" suggests that the priest does not really want to hold up the happy proceedings with a boring piece of legal necessity so, it almost appears, he disowns responsibility for the remark—he does not "require", but is himself "required" by someone else or by the abstract legal procedure.

The Prayer Book talks of marriage as, "instituted of God" and "adorned and beautified by Christ's presence and first miracle he wrought at Cana of Galilee". In the new service, gone is the adorning and beautifying along with the miracle, and we are left with the bathetic, "... the presence of our Lord Jesus Christ with those celebrating a wedding". But there is nothing of the spirit of Christ at this feast, and the omission of the miraculous story about the water turned into wine severs the connection between the ceremony in church and the mystical union that is betwixt Christ and his church.

In the Prayer Book's Solemnisation of Matrimony, there are six words each of one syllable which carry the whole meaning and purpose of the marriage vow: "With this ring I thee wed." These words go back to the time of Chaucer when the bride and groom made their vows at the church door. They are magnificently simple. And they exactly fit the movement of the ring on to the bride's finger. This is liturgical drama at its most spiritually uplifting. This is language, as Ezra Pound said of all great poetry, "charged with meaning to the greatest possible extent". With unbelievable crassness, the revisers have replaced these wonderful and tender words with, "I give you this ring as a sign of our marriage." Eleven words attempt to do the work of what six did unsurpassably. But think for a moment about the logic of this particular desecration: if the groom has to *tell* the bride that the ring is a sign, it means that the sign isn't working. And that is a theological failure.

It is disappointing when the Liturgical Commission, having asked for comments and criticism of their revisions, ignores such criticisms when they are made. I pointed out to the Commissioners not just the literary infelicitousness of the sentence "I give you this ring as a sign of our marriage" but that this extravagant paraphrase enfeebles the sign—like someone explaining a joke. But there it remains on the page where it guarantees that wedding couples will continue to utter it and so make fools of themselves. So Pelagian evasiveness and coy euphemisms are followed by a sentence devoid of meaning.

All the great rites of passage in the Prayer Book were created to deal with the unavoidable crises faced by all human beings—the judgement that we face all the day long. These services are successful and they work theologically because they never underestimate the awfulness of these crises. The Public Baptism of Infants tells us that we are born in Original Sin and then goes on to provide the antidote which is the mystical washing away of sin by the power of the Holy Spirit by the sacramental means of holy water. The Public Baptism of Infants is an example of a desperate situation rescued by desperate measures. But Common Worship's Initiation Services do not recognise this particular crisis and one is left wondering what the service is for. The impression is of firing with blank cartridges. The Solemnisation of Matrimony in the Prayer Book fearlessly scrutinises the fickleness of human sexual feelings and the unruliness of the passions, and then prescribes the cure (one might even say the prophylactic) in that resounding and plain-speaking Introduction: the "remedy against sin". Because the Prayer Book holds an accurate and un-illusioned view of human nature—the same human nature, incidentally, that was noted in The Public Baptism of Infants to be corrupted by Original Sin—it is able to provide a rite of passage which is appropriate to the occasion. The Prayer Book also provides a funeral service, The Burial of the Dead, which is nothing short of miraculous in the way it produces glory out of decay. But it is able to do this only by staring steadfastly into the decay in the first place.

The Prayer Book's Burial of the Dead service rang out its words of magnificent defiance: "I know that my Redeemer liveth and that he shall stand upon the earth at the latter day, and though worms destroy this body yet in my flesh shall I see God." Words of faith made more faithful by their association with the triumphant aria from Handel's *Messiah*. But this marvellous encouragement finds no inclusion here because the euphemistic liturgical processes that produced Common Worship will certainly not mention such nasty things as worms. Modernising liturgists who could not bring themselves to mention the flesh when it was animated (in The Marriage Service) will hardly dare speak of it when it is deceased. No "vile bodies" either. What, corpses at funerals—whatever next? But because Common Worship avoids the stark presentation of the fact and terror of death, the comfort and reassurance it tries to give is weakened. In Common Worship The Funeral Service is dislocated from the event whose terror it is meant to answer. It is therefore unreal. For example, in the Prayer Book the "vile body" is mentioned so that in the very next line we can be reassured that at the general resurrection God will change it "that it may be like unto his glorious body." Because the squeamish Common Worship omits the vileness, it is obliged to leave out the glory as well. We are offered instead, "who will transform our frail bodies." In my dictionary "vile" is said to mean, "worthless, morally base, depraved, shameful, abject". "Frail" means only "fragile, in weak health"—just like Common Worship's Funeral Service in fact. Again I have discussed this issue with liturgical revisers and they say they cannot believe that the human body is vile. They do not seem to see what the vileness in question entails. It is not that there is something rotten about human flesh—though, of course, given the chance, corpses do rot: the vileness referred to in The Burial of the Dead is a moral vileness—"who for our sins art justly displeased"—and, in fact, the same corruption and decadence of the human person indicated in The Public Baptism of Infants and The Solemnisation of Matrimony.

Perhaps the most disturbing and aweful verse in the whole Bible is the shortest—where St John tells us, "Jesus wept." This is here reproduced as "Jesus Christ was moved to tears"—as if he'd just been watching Leonardo di Caprio and Kate Winslett go down in The Titanic for the umpteenth time. "Jesus wept" is a terrible saying about the nature of the divine compassion, but "was moved to tears" suggests only emotional instability.

There are moments of sheer bathos here which exceed even that found in the baptism and marriage rites. There are two paragraphs "for reading before the service" and they include the phrase, "... there is a real sense of loss at the death of a loved one." Did even the most committed Christian believer suspect there is no such sense? There is also some (unintended?) black humour. In a section headed "Ministry at the Time of Death" it is suggested that the minister might read verses from the Bible to the person who is dying. It then adds, "Wherever possible, care should be taken to use versions of texts familiar to the dying person." So the Liturgical Commission which has dedicated the last three decades to expunging all recollection of the Prayer Book and the Authorised Version from the public's memory, relents at the last and allows us to have the real words when we are dying! Let us give thanks for small mercies. But the very gesture prompts anxiety: I mean, if you happen to hear a clergyman uttering words from the real Bible, then look out—you're very likely to be on your last legs.

In what is probably intended as a reference to the Psalmist's saying, "Thou knowest my downsitting and my uprising, my going out and my coming in" it says, "Lord be with us as we open the door." The mourners will laugh, surely? If only it had said, "Lord be with us as we open the box," we could have imagined we were contestants in a macabre TV quiz show. These examples are not trivial sources of mere amusement: because they arise out of a failure to understand what will go into ordinary English and what will not, they are bound to result in something which is theologically inadequate.

There are prayers which contradict themselves within three lines. In one of these it says, "Although he [God] causes grief..." then immediately goes on to say, "He does not willingly afflict or grieve anyone." So it looks as if God's right hand does not know what his left hand is doing! The plain meaning is that God wills some things unwillingly. Theological feebleness is one thing: theological contradiction is a worse thing altogether. "Before time began" is another example.

Occasionally, the revisers fail to distinguish between words appropriate to a technical theological discussion and words suitable at a religious service. In the Prayers of Penitence it says, "But we have this treasure in earthen vessels to show that the transcendent power belongs to God." The technical word "transcendent" has no place in a religious rite. Besides, is such a technical word thought to be "accessible language" for people supposed to have difficulties with "With this ring I thee wed"? "Though worms destroy this body" has been replaced by the bizarre expression, "After my skin has been destroyed"—what, through sitting too long in the sun? "Bless those who had the care of him/her, especially doctors, nurses and technicians." "Technicians"? This will only make mourners think of mechanism and robotics. Besides it is gratuitously invidious to single out some helpers for mention but not others. If technicians are to get a round of applause together with the doctors and nurses, then let's hear it for the taxi-driver, the ward-cleaner and the chef. Further echoes of the New Age resound in a prayer that begins with the clumsy and inappropriate invocation, "Intimate God" and descends to the sub-Freudian, "Reconcile us through your cross to all we have rejected in ourselves." Bad theology again: for there are things in ourselves which we ought to reject—sin, for example. Then "As we remember our death ...." As Tommy Cooper might have said, "It's a nice trick if you can do it!"

The authors of Common Worship have made an effort to provide funeral rites fitting for specific occasions—sundry kinds of death. There is The Order for the Funeral of a Child and there are prayers to be said following a suicide or after a violent death. The Funeral of a Child begins with the sentence, "We meet in the faith that death is not the end, and may be faced without fear, bitterness or guilt." Certainly the gospel proclaims that death is not the end, but can it really be faced without fear? A very few extremely brave people may come to regard death with equanimity and to stand fast against its pains; but that is not what Scripture means when it speaks of the fear of death. Death is to be feared not because it is likely to be physically painful, but because it is the prelude to God's judgement. Perhaps we might face death without "bitterness"—though the Prayer Book offers the real meaning of the bitterness involved when it says, "Deliver us from the bitter pains of eternal death"—but we should not approach death without feeling guilty, for the very good reason that we *are* guilty. I think I can see what the revisers are laudably trying to do in this opening sentence: they mean to reassure the distraught parents that the death of their child is not their fault. But that message would be best given in the sermon instead of in a well-meaning but theologically confused opening sentence.

There is a prayer to be said *after a violent death* and it includes the words: "... that we may treasure the memory of his life more than the manner of his death." This is meant to be the sort of thing that can be said after a fatality on the roads or even after a murder, but the language is uncertain and so the theology is confused. It asks that we "treasure" the memory of the life "more than" the manner of the death. What is this "more than"? Surely we should not treasure the manner of his death *at all*? Of course, prayers do teach theology but when too much—questionable teaching?—is attempted, then we risk the composition of a prayer that seems to be offering instruction to God in the ways of human psychology:

> We find it hard to forgive the deed that has brought us so much grief.
> But we know that, if life is soured by bitterness, an unforgiving spirit brings no peace ....

The psychological understanding here is fallacious and so the theology is misleading. Apart from the connotations of modern therapeutics in "if life is soured by bitterness", where once again we are not far from the counselling clinic, there is surely room for bitterness. Suppose the violent death was the hacking to death of your wife by a mad axeman while you were on your honeymoon. Are you not allowed to feel some bitterness? If you did not, you would hardly be human. This prayer seems to be saying that you should not harbour these natural and legitimate bitter feelings, and so it does not answer the grief of the occasion. It would have been better to frame a prayer that offered the bitterness to God for it is not we ourselves through our own strenuous efforts who can provide consolation: it is God alone who can wipe away all tears from our eyes. Better to ask him then, rather than prescribe self-help to a man beside himself with grief and anger.

The prayer *after a violent death* also includes the words, "It is beyond our understanding and more than we can bear." Perhaps this would be true in the case of the murder of a member of the family, but what if the case was the shooting, by a soldier, of a terrorist who was about to detonate a bomb in a shopping arcade? This would not be "beyond our understanding" and most people would be, if not entirely happy about it, at least relieved that the soldier had acted in time to prevent an atrocity. And even a terrorist should be given a proper funeral.

In the prayer *after a suicide* it says, "Hear our prayer for those in despair." This is too vague to provide any theological guidance or consolation to the mourners. Are "those in despair" meant to be the mourners? What if they are not despairing, but trusting in God? Or is it the person who has taken his own life who is reckoned to be in despair? Why should anyone think that? I think the prayer is meant rather as a generality, as it were, "Following this suicide, let us pray for all those tempted to do away with themselves." But the vagueness of it all produces only confusion and theological inadequacy. The prayer *after a long illness* does not understand the physical and mental pains of someone who takes a long time to die. It says, "Our life is a fleeting shadow that does not endure" whereas to one enduring a prolonged agony, it is much more likely to be experienced as unbearably long drawn out.

Taking account of the perceived weaknesses of the ASB, the revisers have tried to produce a new book with a stronger sense of shared liturgical experience, and this attempt is suggested in the use of the word *Common* in the title. But it is hard to see how this aim will be achieved in a book which contains so many alternative forms. Some thought that the four Eucharistic prayers in ASB were two, or even three, too many: Common Worship has eight. In the Prayer Book, inexpressibly moving, it says "In the same night that he was betrayed, he took bread . . . ." Common Worship's Prayer E says, "He had supper with his friends." The heartbreaking spiritual intensity of Christ's Passion is dissipated by those words which are surely out of context? One could write a summary of those terrible events in their sequence—something like, "He took bread, he was betrayed, he was arrested, mocked, scourged and crucified." The expression "took bread" is continuous with the other events. But to confuse idioms is destructive of the whole spiritual sense. I mean, one could not plausibly write, "He had supper with his friends, he was betrayed, arrested etc." Having supper with friends does not belong in the same contextual universe as being crucified, whereas "took bread" does.

Those eight Eucharistic prayers are clumsy and wordy. Prayer B for example contains the tautologous phrase, ". . . and revealed the resurrection by rising to new life." How could that be an improvement on a familiar direct affirmation such as, "On the third day he rose again"? This Prayer B is highly subjective and even receptionist in its theology of what is actually going on when the Eucharist is celebrated. It asks only that ". . . these gifts of bread and wine may be *to us* [my italics] the body and blood of Our Lord Jesus Christ". This prayer also declares that the Eucharist is a "memorial" and as such it is designed with low churchmen in mind. Other of the prayers reflect the catholic tradition—but the glory of Cranmer's one original prayer was that it could be (and was and is) used satisfactorily by representatives of all the different parties in the Church of England. Prayer F claims that God reveals "... the power of [your] love made perfect in our human weakness". This is misleading. God's love was not made perfect *in* our human weakness but to atone *for* it by the perfection of Christ's sacrifice.

The Creed—or, as it is here described, one of the "Authorised Affirmations of Faith"—perpetuates a serious error which first occurred in the ASB. God is described as maker of all that is "seen and unseen". The traditional Creed says "visible and invisible" and the two phrases are not interchangeable. You cannot see the Holy Ghost because He is invisible; but you cannot see the marmalade only because it is behind the toast rack. Once again a flawed understanding of the meaning of ordinary English produces misleading theology. There are more serious theological errors. For example, in another of these Authorised Affirmations it says, "For as mind and body form one human being, so the one Christ is both divine and human." Yes, he is both divine and human, but not in the sense implied by this affirmation: that Christ's mind is divine but his body human. The doctrine of Nicaea is that the whole person of Christ is both human and divine. This revision of traditional orthodoxy smacks of Docetism. The Prayer Book's version of the Nicene Creed declares that Christ was "begotten of his Father before all worlds" whereas Common Worship has "eternally begotten of the Father" which is not the meaning of the original Greek. One might think that The Daily Missal got this admittedly difficult piece of doctrine as right as anyone could expect without lessening the mystery in its "Et ex Patre natum omnia saecula". The concept of eternal begetting, by comparison, is barely intelligible.

But how are we even to expect intelligence and coherence after we have read the Introduction to Common Worship's Holy Communion rites? For the parish priest's guidance the Commission says, "What is it that this community wishes to emphasise as it celebrates the Eucharist?" As a theological principle, this is wrong from the start: the Eucharist is not the scenario for our emphases, but a representation in the here and now of Christ's great act of self-consecration. It is not something which provides a theme for self-expression, as if the congregation were a class of primary school children under instruction from a thoroughly modern teacher whose desire is that they "express themselves". The Holy Communion is not about self-expression, local or personal emphases and whims, but a solemn re-enactment of the institution of the Sacrament. Another question in the Introduction asks, "How will you present the celebration so that the deep structure of the rite is clear?" This theological hybrid seems to derive from Chomsky's transformational grammar—out of Gregory Dix. Then, "How will you try to secure a different feel for the Eucharist at different seasons?" The untheological word "feel" is a continuation of the touchy feely language we came across in The Marriage Service.

There is a section called "Schedule of permitted variations to The Book of Common Prayer orders for Morning and Evening Prayer where these occur in Common Worship": a slim section but replete with theological feebleness and plenty of mistakes. For example, "Your Son our Saviour was born in poverty in a manger." He was not born in a manger.

He was born of his mother and *laid* in a manger. In this phrase, "born in poverty in a manger" the political opinions of the revisers are too apparent and they might seem to derive more from the Left-leaning Board of Social Responsibility than from students of historical theology. Our Lord was not born in poverty: his earthly father Joseph was a tradesman and of the middle class. Besides, the circumstances of Jesus' birth are irrelevant to the truth of the Incarnation—that greatest of all condescensions. The Liturgical Commission seems to think that for God to be born in relative poverty is somehow a greater condescension than if he had been born Mayor of Stockport—or even if he had chosen to be born as Napoleon or the Czar of all the Russias. That the Second Person of the Holy Trinity chose to be born at all is, of course, the miracle. The revisers do not seem to be able to imagine the great gulf that exists between the infinite, almighty and everlasting God and ourselves, frail children of dust and feeble as frail. The same political leanings are evident in the Harvest Prayer in which we are asked to confess "the sins of our society".

Prayers for Various Occasions reveals a radical shift in the perceived order of precedence as the bishops pray for themselves before they pray for the Queen. In the Prayer Book the Queen, as Supreme Governor of the Church of England comes first in the list of petitions. In the ASB Her Majesty came second. But now in Common Worship's most recent demotion, she comes ninth. One suspects a creeping republicanism, a suspicion not dissolved by the following prayer for "members of the European Institutions". In all this, what might at first appear to be a minor adjustment we see a profound shift in theological understanding. It is not a matter of no importance that the bishops put themselves above the

Queen but a fundamental change in the understanding of what the Church of England is. For the Prayer Book the monarch is Supreme Governor who appoints the bishops. To put the bishops before the Queen is therefore to announce a change in the order of authority: the bishops are masters now and the monarch is prayed for only out of courtesy.

The Alternative Service Book 1980, always thought of rather like contemporary consumer durables, expected to wear out in a few years, was originally licensed for only ten years but survived for twenty, and so may be thought to have served its purpose. At the same time, ASB was propaganded in 1980 as the Church's greatest publishing event in 300 years, and if it had seized the minds and hearts of the faithful it could surely have been expected to last more than one twentieth as long as the Book of Common Prayer has so far done.

In the Commission's Introduction to Common Worship entitled *Planning for Change: Suggestions and Ideas* reprinted above it says, "When the ASB was published, no one knew which (if any) of the new services would stand the test of time."[3] Twenty years: it is an eccentric notion of what constitutes the test of time. Cranmer's book has stood that test for four hundred and fifty years.

We must have some sympathy with the task facing the revisers. They could not ignore the comprehensive failure of the ASB to halt the catastrophic decline in church attendance during the period of its issue. Something had to be done. But what? I suggest that the best thing would have been for them not to labour over the production of yet more

[3] P. 50, above.

and lengthier alternatives but to recommend the parishes to return to the Prayer Book which throughout is theologically superior to both the ASB and Common Worship.

IX

The Prayer Book and the Modern World

Peter Mullen & Ian Robinson

> Blessed is the man whose strength is in thee: in whose heart are thy ways.
>
> Who going through the vale of misery use it for a well: and the pools are filled with water.[1]

Earlier in this book Professor MacCulloch has given us a panoramic sketch of the history of the Book of Common Prayer, and Professor Homan and Professor Martin have looked, from different standpoints, at the history of its partial replacement during the last half century. We conclude with another sketch, as it has to be, from a different perspective, that will make stand out one basic problem which, we believe, the Liturgical Commission has been unable to solve.

There is no serious challenge to the view that Cranmer's liturgical prose is very good, and that in sentence structure and rhythm it is also distinctively modern, compared either with much of the contemporary humanist prose mentioned by Professor MacCulloch or with the good workaday

[1] Psalm lxxxiv. 5–6, Prayer Book version.

medieval prose, consisting largely of strings of simple sentences, which it succeeded. But Cranmer's prose is not quite the modern prose which, one might say without exaggeration, has made our world.

Modern English prose became a common possession, with remarkable suddenness, in the 1660s. The decade of the restoration of King Charles II, the decade of what many of his party hoped and expected to be general reaction, brought in what we recognize, by calling it the Age of Reason, as an age quite different from the age of religious conflict it succeeded. The belief that reason and religion are inimical, which would have seemed strange in earlier ages, is one of its marks. And "reason" understood in the Restoration way is incarnate in modern prose.

When Bishop Sprat or Bishop Wilkins or Dr John Locke were told, as sometimes happened, that the tendency of their work was anti-religious, they were understandably indignant, though they might have borne with greater equanimity the charge that they were anti-poetic. The Enlightenment in this country was largely the work of bishops the sincerity of whose professions we have no reason to doubt, and did not Locke publish *The Reasonableness of Christianity*? The eighteenth century in England was, however, at least not like the sixteenth in that its literature was not Shakespearean and its prose not Cranmerian.

T. S. Eliot's name for the great change of the 1660s was "the dissociation of sensibility". Some modern academics say that they can find no sense in the phrase; indeed to say so is a kind of membership ticket of a yet more "post-modern" world: but it names a thing, visible to the naked eye of anyone who reads Shakespeare's *Antony and Cleopatra* and then Dryden's reworking *All for Love, or, the World Well*

Lost,[2] or who goes straight from a reading of the collects in the Book of Common Prayer to Bishop Sprat's *History of the Royal Society*. An age of terrible religious wars, of which our own civil war is a comparatively benign example, of great tragic drama on stage too, is succeeded by an age of "reason, truth and nature" to which nothing could be more stupid than fighting

> like mad or drunk
> For Dame Religion as for punk

and which had no tragic drama at all, but a generation of profound and brilliant natural scientists and mathematicians. Modern science itself originated, for instance in the so civil writing of Boyle, in a reaction against the rule of the saints.

The enormously solid good sense of the Age of Reason is also enormously limited. Its nemesis appeared in the form of the horses of Book IV of *Gulliver's Travels*, whose "reason" removes so much of necessary humanity that it drives Gulliver clinically insane. "What is Whiggery?" asks Yeats:

> A ... rational sort of mind
> That never looked out of the eye of a saint
> Or out of a drunkard's eye.[3]

Anybody who thinks of human life as having to do with saints and sinners as well as sensible people, with poetry as well as well-conducted argument, with seeing visions, dreaming dreams, with "ecstasies, and agonies, and love", will have difficulty in saying so in the prose of the Enlightenment. The whole romantic movement makes the judgement, without displacing prose-and-reason.

[2] Cf. F. R. Leavis, *English Literature in Our Time and the University*, 1969, pp. 91–2 and *Education and the University*, 2nd edn, 1948, pp. 48 ff., and discussions in C. J. Purvis, *The Offensive Art*, Brynmill Press, 1991.
[3] "The Seven Sages".

And then (for this history has to be much potted) as Yeats also observes,

> Locke sank into a swoon;
> The Garden died;
> God took the spinning-jenny
> Out of his side

and commonsense-with-science took the form of the industrial revolution, the mechanized organization of societies, then the information revolution and the present day.

The Age of Reason launched (in England; France was rather earlier) in the 1660s was very homogeneous, with a strong positive culture we are identifying with modern prose. The reliability of English prose of the eighteenth century is much like that of almost all contemporary craftsmanship, architecture and town planning. Things were well and carefully made, neat, convenient, elegant, and though individually and by hand, with reliable standards. It is as hard to find a badly proportioned Georgian house as a badly constructed Augustan sentence. There is a general elegance that even rises to beauty, as in the terraces and crescent of Bath. But there in the middle, essential to the whole city, is the Abbey, proclaiming something not bounded by reason, truth and nature, at least as solid as the Pump Room but giving a hint of heaven that even Wren was incapable of. The whole age is actually only completed when one sees such opposites as an element.

Any genuine spirit of an age is always made out of conflict. No conflict, no spirit, and we then have one of those terrible times which Spengler observed in cultures that had run their course; when nothing changes and "art", philosophy, religion are condemned to endless repetition. The closest example to us in time is the Roman Empire, the fag end of the great classical age, in the three hundred years before Christianity was accepted and began leavening the lump from the inside. What saved the Enlightenment from the state of irredeemable fixity in a severely selective "reason" was poetry and religion, surviving and developing from an earlier age. Let us not forget that it was the eighteenth century which established Shakespeare, who went clean against all the age's canons of taste, as a great national possession and fact of the language.

The very decade of the establishment of our modern prose world was also that of *Paradise Lost*, *The Pilgrim's Progress* and, anticipating all the other developments by a couple of years, the conservatively reformed Book of Common Prayer; whose prose is modern but not that of the new age. Throughout the eighteenth century Bunyan was read in the cottages, Cranmer in all the Wren churches; there was that degree of amalgamation of two ages. One of the most remarkable facts about the Age of Reason was that no serious effort was made to replace the English Bible with a modern translation. The 1611 Bible was as far from the predominant ethos of 1750 as it is from ours; it went on in the Age of Reason more or less as what Coleridge called the Christian Church, "the *sustaining, correcting, befriending* Opposite of the world".[4]

In the same decade that Hume wrote his *Four Dissertations* beginning with "The Natural History of Religion", so beautifully lucid and so impervious to religion! Charles Wesley was creating the great Christian hymnody of the language. The Age of Reason also saw John Wesley stumping the country preaching "scriptural holiness", the

[4] *On the Constitution of the Church and State*, 1830, ed. John Barrell, 1972, p. 98.

scripture in question being the King James Bible undumbed.

Our wonderful, endlessly fascinating nineteenth century gave us a new kind of wealth, the railways, the dark Satanic mills, utilitarianism and the religion of humanity: also universal education in which the Bible and religious observance were an important part, as was, thanks to Matthew Arnold, English poetry. As well as the (now closed) Temples of Reason, the nineteenth century saw the culmination of a parish pattern first sketched by Cranmer, of church, hall, rectory and school. The nineteenth century was, perhaps, the greatest age of the Book of Common Prayer and the one that made so many Prayer Book phrases proverbial. The Tractarians and Evangelicals both used the Prayer Book as a matter of course, though they had their different reservations about it.

Right down to the mid twentieth century the Prayer Book, the Bible and the hymns principally of the Wesleys and Watts provided the religious language of the whole nation, including nonconformists, Romans and those who rejected religion, the heirs of the Enlightenment and its prose. The Bloomsbury Group, so influential on English letters, were completely impervious to religion. That did not prevent Virginia Woolf or Leonard Woolf from using biblical phraseology when they needed.

The twentieth century had its poets and novelists too, of whom at least one, D. H. Lawrence, was of Shakespearean habit. Lawrence, a lapsed Congregationalist who in adult life had something of the Bloomsbury obliviousness to Christianity, though he hated Bloomsbury because he thought it irreligious, simply could not have done his work except in the same language as that of the English Bible and the Book of Common Prayer. This is as straightforwardly true as the common observation that Aeschylus could not have written his plays, so different in sensibility and form, except as "slices from Homer's banquet".

We show ourselves heirs of the Age of Enlightenment whenever we use ordinary prose, that is, every day; but the descent might well have taken another form. The Whig lords cannot be held responsible for the 1960s. It is hard enough to imagine religion or poetry in the post-Enlightenment managerial prose that makes so great a fraction of our world, but what to say of the decline of democracy into the Age of Pop? Hume, Locke, Boyle, are after all distinguished names; their various differences with religion were a serious matter. After the 1960s the tendency is against seriousness altogether.

The eighteenth century had its faults, but they did not include dumbing down. Taste was so secure partly because it was so firmly governed by a very self-confident class of gentry and aristocracy, able to enforce their taste everywhere. The first assertion in the American Declaration of Independence, that all men are born free and equal, was made by gentlemen who had no intention of conceding equality of taste to their servants or their labourers. We do see here, though, one of the early signs of a contemporary phenomenon, the assertion of equality made on authority by a class which has no intention of surrendering its power.

We now really believe, or say we do, in the equality of everything whatever. Just as all people are equal, though some happen to be much richer than others, so are all kinds of music, "from avant-garde pop and industrial noise to classical music and jazz".[5] The National Theatre performs indifferently Shakespeare and *Oklahoma*. In our greatly expanded universities all subjects are equal, Mathematics and Pig Enterprise Management, Philosophy and Promotion of Fashion and Fashion Design, and all equally, we think, will equip us for the competitive world of the third millennium. Study English literature and all authors will be equal. After a phase when, to be modern, architecture had to be based on undisguised steel frames, new buildings are an eclectic mixture of style revivals, including for domestic buildings a popular set of Victorian styles, though none would ever be mistaken for originals. Every style is the equal of every other.

It is the same with "sexual orientation": a "gay" lifestyle is no better and no worse than marriage, though perhaps equality does not stretch as far as celibacy, which is distinctly not of the age; and, rather mysteriously, there is universal condemnation of "child abuse".

The perpetual assertion of multiculturalism, itself a feature of the age, has to follow if we have many cultures and they are all equal; but here we meet a few very odd things. Can multiculturalism be something all cultures have in common even if cultures are distinct from one another? Multiculturalism, too, in this egalitarian society, is always asserted on authority by its cultural leaders, who are not themselves multicultural.

There are two senses of *multicultural.* We have some ghettoes, and the other year a government minister was scandalized to discover that in one of them arranged marriages were being made and girls punished for unchastity,

[5] *The Financial Times* 20 May 2000, p. II; an article subtitled "Ludovic Hunter-Tilney on the South Bank Centre's love affair with pop".

that is, it did not belong to the modern world; in this sense multiculturalism is just a juxtaposition of uncomprehendingly different groups. The multiculturalism offered as a common faith by our establishment is something different, demanding more give and take, more of a mix. The idea seems to be that one culture is made out of sharing many. About this there is one prominent oddity. For though the faith is constantly proclaimed, to the disinterested observer (from the U.S.A., for instance) neither we nor the French nor the Germans appear to live in a really multicultural society. The unicultural sameness of "the media" can seem, indeed, oppressive in a way not possible to the Victorian Age or before; for the mass media, unknown before in the world, have made possible a uniformity eagerly realized by our communicators.

Even at best, the composition of liturgy in the best prose of the modern and post-modern world, as against the prose of the Cranmer tradition, is not going to be straightforward. Where, by the way, would be go for distinguished modern prose? Iris Murdoch's novels? Mr Blair's speeches? or Mr Hague's? Perhaps the standard is set by *Times* editorials or the annual reports of limited liability companies, which the typography of Common Worship does follow? With *Producing Your Own Orders of Service*, August 2000, however, the Church is evidently trying to get right into the modern world as commonly understood, the world of pop. The anxiety to be intelligible is now veering in that direction. And if our formal modern prose is the hangover of a world in which liturgy is difficult, what to say of the successor?

In practice, both equality and multiculturalism now just mean the the world of the mass media. Houyhnhnmland must have been a boring place, but not as stunningly[6] dull as this one.

To test this contention just go to the radio and twiddle the knob from one end of the waveband to the other: the overwhelming saturation is a noise, alien indeed to the eighteenth century, called "pop"; station after station indistinguishable. If you want evidence of a world where everything is new, yet endlessly repetitive, need you go further? Yet when the authorities are asked for a wider slot for Radio Three we are told the waveband is already full. Even on Radio Three there is too much repetitive jazz and Peruvian nose flute music, everything presented with sickly smartness and brightness such as in real life makes you want to hit people; one after another lachrymose sentimentalist such as Fergal Keane coming on to present their choice of music.

But radio is of course the junior partner of television. Saturday evening on the main BBC1 is *Jim's Full Vacuity* followed by *Spot the Moron* followed by the intellectual challenge of the *National Lottery Live*—which is indistinguishable from the National Lottery Dead—followed by fake blood and pretend sex in the medical dramas. Then there are the soap operas. They may be Australian with all those beautiful young people who somehow seem to be animated waxworks. If home-produced they give the impression—watched by more than half the adult population every week—that life consists of package holidays and child-abuse relieved by bouts of glue-sniffing and incest. In their cast-lists there is not one single intelligent or interesting character. "Family viewing", it's called. But all the families here are dysfunctional. As on radio, all the documentaries are introduced by a snarl of pop music, and even the BBC news

[6] *Stunning* is now a commonly used term of approbation.

begins to a disco Greenwich time signal. Often the nasty "music" continues right through the programmes, even the Schools programmes, but especially the holiday programmes consisting of Sharon telling you how much she drank at Teneriffe or how much Doug enjoyed the lap-dancers in Las Vegas.

Even when they go on a "classics" holiday there is no history or culture: the presenters, scared stiff of appearing "élitist", follow the blundering tourists by day, the limit of whose brain power it is to ask, "How old is it?", and the drug-crazed clubbers by night. No need to fear élitism. They're about as élitist as Sid the Sexist and the Fat Slags in *Viz*. This is all called "fun": object and you are square or uncool.

And the people participate, or form "an invited audience" —but what would an uninvited audience do?—to listen to or participate in discussions of social problems: wife-beating, alcoholism, religious sects and cults etc. Sheila from Sheffield is having an affair with her grandad. Brian from Bognor thinks it would be sexy to have a leg amputated. What does the audience say? Anything emotionally stultifying and intellectually banal. Bread and circuses, they produce and elicit uninformed and unreflective responses, self-indulgent, embarrassing, childish. Then there are the shows in studied bad taste like *Blind Date*, in which individuals are regarded only as objects of others' satisfactions. This goes right against a fundamental early lesson which we try to teach our children in real life: that human beings are not to be treated as means to an end but as ends in themselves.

Children's television, though, is all whirling captions and loud-mouthed presenters shrieking in an English with hardly any consonants at youngsters in the "studio audience" who win small prizes for shrieking back. The subject matter: pop music and personalities. David Beckenham and Posh Spice. This too is officially "fun" and run by the department of "light entertainment", not a bad disguise for the Prince of Darkness. It is banal. St Thomas Aquinas said that banality is evil. The precise evil here is child-abuse in the well-recognised form of a refusal to give the children what can really nourish them. It is not kindness to deprive children of culture and sensitivity. Take them to the cinema instead and they will see the wonderful world of Disney, produced by letting powerful European fairy-tales go to America and then buying them back denatured and schmalzified.

Well, turn off the box, leave the cinema, and go and find something to read. But look in an ordinary newsagent for a modestly serious weekly, as seriousness is understood on *The Spectator* or *The New Statesman*, and where will you find it in the ranks of special-interest glossies, computer magazines, mild pornography and gossip about pop music and personalities?

They do have newspapers, so pick up one, then *lasciate ogni speranza*. Acres of the same consumer drivel to which is added a daily catalogue of health obsessions and a more extensive "showbiz" catalogue with pictures and stories of which celebs are bonking which other celebs. We are the people, and so we all want to know that an overblown footballer wears his wife's (she is a "singer") knickers. All this in the "heavies" as well as the tabloids. The Fashion Editor of *The Daily Telegraph* writes, "A creative sensation was achieved when the models had their names written on their blouses." The Music Correspondent of *The Times* writes, "If Shakespeare were alive today, he would be writing soaps and

Beethoven would be on 'E' writing dance music." He would, that is, be uniculturally the same as anyone else, and his music would top the pops for a week or two.

Or let your eyes fall on one of the more recent consumer-cum-new-age fads.

> While fewer than five per cent of housebuyers bother to invest in a structural survey, a growing number are spending hundreds of pounds checking the flow of chi.[7]

People avoid house numbers with "four" in them because, as we are informed by the *Times* correspondent, "The word 'four' in Chinese means 'death'." In English the word "rubbish" means "rubbish". How right Chesterton was when he said, "When men stop believing in God, they do not believe in nothing, they believe in anything"!

Schools, no doubt, provide the remedy to this nonsense: EDUCATION, EDUCATION, EDUCATION. But the man who made that his winning election cry also said that the Millennium Dome, the perfect incarnation of the "modern", is an educational experience. For education too is fun. History is fun, *The Times* told us recently. Fun can be remarkably grim, especially when the history is subordinated to what is politically correct, as we glance at bits of the past to enjoy our own superiority.

Go to the bookshop then? But most best-selling contemporary fiction is infantile. George Eliot was a best seller in her day: in George Eliot real characters face difficult moral problems. In the modern best-seller the crudely sketched stereotypes are "hunky" or "drop-dead gorgeous"; they proceed through a series of unlikely adventures. The impression is of one very long car chase or animated cartoon.

[7] *The Times*, 22 January 2000.

Sexual exploits are *de rigueur* even in Mills & Boon but they are invariably written in such a way as inadvertently to produce laughter or incredulity—as if the author, armed with a thesaurus, was trying to describe acrobats and contortionists. They are written for moral and emotional illiterates and no effort is made to educate them—adults who are really unschooled children. The emotional and psychlogical range is what we would expect of infants without the fresh imagination of infants. And their deepest thoughts and feelings are depressingly shallow and trivial: is he going to be able to bed this woman and is she going to come in to a lot of money?

The writing looks not merely as if it has been produced *for* uneducated people but *by* them. There is, for all the appearance of vacuous excitement, an obligatory pedestrian style without which the prose would not be published and which reminds us of the child's reading manual. People "croak hoarsely," "murmur softly" and "strongly insist." This is Noddy language. When a novelist employs language like this in trying to present serious issues the whole project is bound to collapse. But the sales hold up. By sales volume this is the language of the age.

Turning then to public life. There was a time when public figures were regarded for their occasional forays into light-hearted public relations: the mayor might be Father Christmas or the bishop sit in the stocks at the garden fête in order to raise money for charity. Now we are always at the fête or the pantomime. Not only local government figureheads and ecclesiastical dignitaries, but would-be serious politicians and statesmen play the fool on every conceivable occasion in their attempts to catch the cameras. When she was Northern Ireland Secretary "Mo" Mowlam put pop before politics and was rewarded by political popularity. Pop culture is essentially infantile and yet even the Prime Minister is happiest—or at least he is happiest when being photographed—alongside pop stars and "celebrities". This degrades and demeans public life by suggesting that government itself requires some extraneous justification of its authenticity. Worse, by association it exalts the childish preoccupations of our society above the business and institutions of government. In currently popular phrase, the government has to be seen to be "cool"—which means trivial and infantile. Parliament itself is turned into a sort of show every Wednesday afternoon by Prime Minister's Question time, shown live on television, in which the last election and the next are fought weekly in a kind of eternity that brings us back to Spengler's limbo of endless repetition.

These are symptoms of an enfeebled national character, as if the object of our culture were to produce a race of morons ... the Age of Reason suffering from senile decay. Britain has become the thick man of Europe. Intelligence, criticism, rational discussion are everywhere rejected in favour of a vacuous and unsatisfying pursuit of "fun", as in "This is a fun programme ... a fun presentation ... a fun experience." All fun is equal. It makes an age "all of a piece, like madness".

It is enough to make a man turn to religion ...

So you open the Bible—only it's the Good News Bible, the religious equivalent of Mills & Boon romance. Everything is low-key sugary:

> Mary stood crying outside the tomb. While she was still crying, she bent over and looked in the tomb and saw two angels there dressed in white, sitting where the body of Jesus had been, one at the head and the other

> at the feet. "Woman, why are you crying?" they asked her.[8]

This is so like Megan visiting the Baptist Cemetery. "Within the garden of Remembrance she found a small plaque with her mother's name engraved on it, and the words "I Miss You' half hidden behind an enormous vase of orchids and lilies. It was immensely poignant and immensely moving.' "[9] Oh no it wasn't. The last thing the reader of M&B wants is to be really moved. We are not expected, either, actually to *believe* Mills & Boon, and it is asking a bit much to demand that of the Good News Bible.

If liturgy is of the age, this is the age it is of. "I tire," Bishop Stancliffe understandably complains, "of the Church's worship shouldering all the blame for the loss of literary resonances in an age governed by mass-media pressures in general and television in particular." [10] Yes, but is an age so governed a party the Church really wants to gatecrash? *Producing Your Own Orders of Service* makes the comparison mandatory, though Bishop Stancliffe's introductory comment that personal computers and photocopiers have "fed and enabled adaptability to the local context" is still in the comparatively upmarket non-prose we noticed from the Bishop of Guildford, for how do you feed adaptability? and will it bite? The text, however, gives us the authentic dumbing.

Sub-heads are recommended. At the beginning of a service, for instance, it is not enough to say "The Lord be with you": the text should preface that greeting with the headline "The Greeting". In case even that redundant phrase should

[8] John xx.11–13a; *Good News Bible: Today's English Version*, British Usage edn, 1976, p. 146.
[9] Anne Mather, *Sinful Pleasures*, Mills & Boon, 1998, p. 86.
[10] *Model and Inspiration*, p. 23.

prove too difficult for the sort of visitors who will misunderstand "fellow men" we are told to print beside it in the margin, in a big oblong box, "We say 'Hello'." On the next page the ancient and beautiful service of Compline, renamed "Night Prayer", is subtitled "Debriefing the Day with God". Then we get to confession, sub-headed "Dishing the dirt on ourselves". We are not making this up! as some unlucky congregations may expect to confirm soon.

"Dishing the dirt on ourselves" surely expresses, if nothing else, the Church's determination to be of that particular modern world we have glanced at. It does not follow that the efforts are successful by their own standards. The compilers are no more competent at pop-expression than at the composition of collects. They get no further than the Hollywood idiom of the 1930s; and then misuse it at that. When the gangster or his moll *dished the doit* (related to "can dish it out but can't take it"?) they intended revenge. The Church presumably still intends to offer us the hope of mercy.

Nothing worth saying can be said in this style.

The age, whether in its descent from the Enlightenment, in the surviving prose of the broadsheet newspapers, or in the new revelation of the pop world: how can religion be possible in any of the varieties of the language of this age?

Ought not the Church to be leavening this very doughy lump, not trying (however unsuccessfully) to be part of it? The Church has always tried to keep herself unspotted from the world, and to redeem the world. If the Church tries to shack up with this world (even if the world isn't having any), is it surprising that the results are at best dull and at worst deadly? The Church has to oppose this particular world tooth and nail, without any reservations and with zero tolerance. Otherwise she finds herself, by way of banality (above, Aquinas), the bride of a well-known personage much less lovely than Christ.

The problem which we believe the Liturgical Commission has failed to solve is the question of what will mix with what.

By the principle of multiculturalism, all religions are equal, and within the Church of England the Book of Common Prayer is on a par with the "contemporary" services, the Authorized Version of the Bible with the Good News Bible. This equality is the very keystone of Common Worship's efforts to restore unity.

For forty years or so the Church of England has suffered much from the divisions between liturgical reformers and traditionalists, and quite genuine divisions, for some are made enthusiastic, or miserable, by the old forms, some by the new. The task the compilers of Common Worship have set themselves, quite deliberately, is to put an end to this unhappy state, firstly by giving equality and parity of esteem to the different modes of worship.

> The intention is to give a clear signal that both have an appropriate place in the worship of the Church of England today. The hope is that this may help to put an end to destructive and draining battles over modern and traditional forms of worship . . . .[11]

Common Worship: Key Points similarly tells us that "The *Common Worship* services are intended to signal an end to any sense that the old and the new are at odds." This goes back to the Liturgical Commission's resolve "to draw the traditions closer together" and "to confirm that the

[11] Above, p. 52.

Church ... needs to provide for a mixture of ancient and modern language."[12]

The end of the history of the reinvention of "common" narrated by Mr Capey, above, seems at this stage of the argument to be a state where to the naked eye two neighbouring congregations practising Common Worship need have hardly anything in common as to their forms of worship. "National uniformity was the declared intention of liturgical policy in the 16th century. The local flexibility built into our new *Common Worship* services is a developed form of the 16th-century assumptions behind the *Book of Common Prayer*," we are told by *Producing Your Own Orders of Service*. How can the inversion of a policy be described as "development" of it? "*Common Worship* emphasises the important part worship plays in expressing our unity." How can it unless the worship has actually something in common? Is not "common" denied by "Your Own"? Equality must be the first defence: they may be different but are "signalled" to be equal and not at odds.

But the line between reuniting and simply recognizing division is not easily drawn.

> Some Principles
> 1 We have recognized and accepted the fact that there is no longer one agreed Eucharistic prayer in the Church of England....
> 2 We have tried to produce texts which are not divisive, in terms of inclusive language, international unity, or theological or churchmanship divisions.[13]

[12] *The Worship of the Church*, 1991, para. 23, p. 10 and para. 73, p. 22; this despite the "vibrant worship", owing "a great deal to *The Alternative Service Book 1980*" that has already "succeeded in uniting the Church liturgically beyond the expectations of many"—despite, in turn, ASB's being "the book that enshrined the breaking of the mould [!] of four hundred years" (para. 46, p. 15).

[13] *Patterns for Worship*, p 12. We note that "churchman" counts as "inclusive".

Other traditions differ; the United Methodists used to extemporize their eucharistic prayers. In the tradition of the Church of England, if there is not one agreed eucharistic prayer is there genuine common worship? If some congregations simply will not use a eucharistic prayer they are in the most obvious sense not in communion with others who will. Some Church of England parishes do not accept that women can validly administer the sacraments. A church which formally includes both those who do and those who do not recognize the validity of the orders of some of that church's own priests might be thought to have taken the principle of "unity by inclusion"[14] as far as it will go. The first hope now is that somehow these mutually exclusive congregations will accept one another.

Producing Your Own Orders of Service does, however, place some limits, which must bring the project into question even at this first stage of tolerance. We are told that service books can go out of date as the ASB "quickly did once inclusive language became an issue in the church." So we should not use in Church such phrases as "fellow men". "Phrases like that are meant to cover both men and women. However, language is not always heard in the way it is intended, and even if *we* know what *we* mean, visitors may not." This strange statement, as well as being insulting and patronising to "visitors", restricts what counts as "common".

> Some parts [of ASB] need to be changed to make it absolutely clear that both men *and* women are being referred to, for example in lines such as, "We have sinned against you and against our *fellow men*" (from the confession in ASB Holy Communion Rite A).[15]

[14] Ninian Comper's phrase quoted by David Stancliffe, *Model and Inspiration*, p. 17.
[15] *Planning for Change*, above, p. 51 .

In Common Worship Order One our fellow men become, in consequence, "our neighbour" (thereby suggesting that we needn't repent of sins against our enemies?) Would anyone in the ordinary world infer from the ASB wording that sins against women don't count? But if this is true of ASB it is surely much truer of the Prayer Book, which naturally uses the ordinary masculine[16] inclusive language. The use of the new "inclusive language" is in fact very divisive. You hold one opinion on this matter or the other. Either you prefer to use the new he/she, (s)he and their vocal equivalents, or you prefer the old inclusive language of all sorts and conditions of men, goodwill towards men, and so on. If the latter is wrong the Liturgical Commission is right not to tolerate it: but then how could "men", by way of the Prayer Book, be part of what we have in common? If not, almost anything counts as "common" *except* the Book of Common Prayer?

The determined preference for he/she, then, seems to half recognize a difficulty. It becomes an insoluble problem, quite unrecognized, when we are told to mix the tolerable and the intolerable.

Since the services in Common Worship, the ASB-derived and the Prayer Book-derived, are plainly of different styles, the hope must be that they will not only co-exist, but mix, and then the mixture itself is what we will have in common, demonstrating the acceptance of all the differences. This would be real multiculturalism in practice, but we should be on the look out for signs that, as with multiculturalism in general, the word may be applied to the predominance of one style.

[16] Masculine is a gender in grammar, male is a sex. *The Worship of the Church* makes the parallel mistake when it talks of "male language" (para. 14, p. 7).

What if the old and the new, as it has seemed to many on both sides, really *are* at odds? Can this mixing of everything really be hoped for as the healing of our divisions? "Can we rejoice in diversity," asks Bishop Stancliffe with some musical vagueness, "finding in rich harmony a greater unity rather than a flat unison?"[17] Doesn't that all depend on whether there is actually harmony, unison (flat, sharp or well-tempered)—or discord?

There are already many churches that alternate between ASB and the Prayer Book, either from week to week or on the same day. Mixtures are frequent within the same service. Some of the most devoted Rite A churches use the "traditional" form of the Lord's Prayer. Conversely Prayer Book Matins or Evensong may end up with prayers in "contemporary" (second-person-plural) idiom. Mixtures are sometimes most obvious with the hymns: *Mission Praise*, for instance, has not-much-edited forms of Victorian and earlier hymns alongside things like

> Lord, I love You,
> You alone did hear my cry;
> You can mend this broken heart of mine.
> Yes, I love You,
> and there is no doubt,
> Lord, You've touched me from the inside out.[18]

and they can frequently be heard in the same service.

The snag is that some things just don't mix. Many women and some men are sensitive about colour clashes. The late Billy Bennett, author of the *Bumper Book of Burlesque Monologues*, used to appear on stage in immaculate dinner jacket and Hawaiian grass skirt. We do not wish to make any

[17] *Model and Inspiration*, p. 23.
[18] No. 432.

close comparison to the mixture in Common Worship, only to assert that the question of what goes with what can be a real one. Medieval parish churches are not even allowed to use modern gypsum-based plaster on the walls!

The barer Rite A–Order One style

> we worship you, we give you thanks,
> we praise you for your glory

achieves its full effect only in the context of familiarity with Cranmer. Without the hostility the words are merely flat. In the other, the new Common Worship style, the collects are quite often Cranmer with the singular turned into the plural and a pompous doxology added. If you know the Prayer Book there is no way of taking either ASB or Common Worship except as criticism or parody of it. The "contemporary" services were brought in specifically to differ from the Prayer Book. If the point of something is to be different, it should not be expected to mix well with what it differs from. If the chalk is brought in so as not to be cheese it is no good expecting a good blend of chalko-cheese. If the "contemporary" services really go well with the Prayer Book they have failed in their purpose.

As a matter of fact, they don't. If the mixture is of incompatibles, the Common Worship wish to "put an end to destructive and draining battles over modern and traditional forms of worship" comes to no more than the wistful wish that things were otherwise. Do stop fighting and respect each other and be good mixers! for the good of the Church!

The composer of new liturgy has only two alternatives. Either he can boldly use what is called "traditional", one of the conditions of which is mastering the style; this is in itself a way of making the traditional contemporary. The most widely used and known liturgical writing of the twentieth century is surely Milner-White's Bidding Prayer added to the Festival of Nine Lessons and Carols made in the late nineteenth century by Bishop Benson of Truro, both "traditional". Or he can even more boldly create something new that will redeem and transform the whole of language. So Dr Pickstock says that

> the revisions [of Vatican II] were simply *not radical enough*. A successful liturgical revision would have to involve a revolutionary re-invention of language and practice which would challenge the structures of our modern world . . . .[19]

This, a tall order, is very like what Cranmer and his generation actually did for the impossibly wandering English prose they found to hand, though, to be sure, they had the advantage of a language and culture religious in its depths. If nothing similar can realistically be claimed for Common Worship, the challenge to the structures of our modern world is still best given by Cranmer. The Prayer Book continues to be the nearest thing this nation has to a general form of the Christian way; beside it ASB and Common Worship are different brands of fudge.

When the Victorians went on about Shakespeare being not for an age but for eternity, perhaps they had a kernel of sense: that the continued recognition of Shakespeare forms the form-of-life. As long as it's recognizably English it will be Shakespearean. So with Cranmer. The replacement of the Book of Common Prayer, though the Church of England has been attempting it for several decades, is not an

[19] Catherine Pickstock, *After Writing*, Oxford, 1998, p. 171.

option. The alternatives to the Prayer Book are "modern" nullity or a new life-form. At present, the former.

If there is to be any survival into the new millennium of England as a Christian nation, with a language in which Christianity can be currently expressed, that language has to grow out of what we have already, and not by way of parody.

Spengler goes wrong when he sees the growth and decay of cultures as a natural, inevitable life cycle. There is nothing inevitable about the triumph of the media-machine or the belief in material progress. English literature, as well as the Bible, is still readable, and you will never find any contributor to either recommending the pursuit of money as a substitute for the pursuit of the good. Our age is made out of mechanism and media but also, still, out of conflict, for the mechanism is not universal. There is still occasional genuine dissent even within the uniculture. What we have been saying is not the opinion of loners, nor of one party; similar things are occasionally heard on left and right.

This is the justification for the term by which the uniculture of the age should be known. Let it be called THE MISERY! The word is used in its ordinary sense, for do the suicide-and-drugs-prone media personalities who are our role-models really look happy? but at the same time precisely in the sense in which we are miserable sinners: merciable, capable of receiving forgiveness. The dissociation of sensibility is itself an aberration, of the family of heresy, which may run its course or may be cured. Not everything can be put together again, but reconstruction is at least as possible as deconstruction. Poetry can still be read, with unpredictable results. So can the Bible. So can the Book of Common Prayer. As long as this can be seen the situation is not irredeemable.

We have to hold fast to that which is good. The Prayer Book, along with what is broadly called literature, lets into our modern life so much sense of a kind we don't otherwise know. It can and does give to life a weight in the age of Nietzsche's "weightlessness". It offers still, as it did in Cranmer's time, the Christian way for this nation. (The Prayer Book is much more likely to be superseded by political change—a French-style secular republic, or European federation—than by linguistic change.) Christians are walkers in a way. But we now, as always, need repentance, the Greek of which means literally a change of mind.

"You can't put the clock back" (though we do that once a year in this country) and "you want the Church to be stuck in a time-warp." Not exactly, though the noble example of the Eastern churches should be kept in mind; their survival of centuries of subordination to kings and emperors and then in some cases seventy years of savage atheistic persecution owes much to their reliable unchangingness. But as a matter of fact the Byzantine way does not seem an option for the West. For all the sameness and fixity of modern life, and *pace* Spengler, it is still true that "Sensibility changes in us all from age to age, whether we will or no." The fixity belongs to those who want to saddle us with the mechanism and thickness of the age, to stick us in the 1960s.

There must have been people in 1659 who said "We can't go back". In fact when we did go back, with the re-adoption of the Prayer Book, a sensibility emerged quite different from that of the age of King Charles I. What new sensibility will grow in the twenty-first century who knows? That can be left to divine inspiration. But if we deny the best of our language, in poetry, in novels, in prayer, there will be no sensibility worth the name to worry about.

Common Worship is in itself a whole set of ready-made practical criticism exercises. Again and again it puts the Prayer Book, the new inauthentic traditional, and the "contemporary", side by side. An exercise we commend to students of English: choose one or two of the new collects in "traditional language" and ask why they are not in traditional language. (The question why the new "contemporary" writing is not idiomatic would be too easy.) Parochial church councils up and down the land will be agonizing about how to replace ASB. All they have to do is put Order One next to Order Two and ask which will place fewer obstacles in the way of the Lord's presence with us.

As we all know, it will not be so simple, partly because Order Two itself does what typography and lineation can to disnature the Prayer Book, but mainly because decisions are not in fact made by serious and well-informed exercises of judgement by church councils. Making the quite large assumption that the PCCs are competent to decide, the priest in charge is, perhaps rightly, very influential, and the liberal establishment, perhaps less rightly, very influential on him or her. The best hope for the survival of the Prayer Book is a genuine change of heart on the part of the powers that be. The present work is offered to the common reader, to members of PCCs, to bishops and clergy, not as propaganda but as provocation to thought. It will give the members of the General Synod a rather different perspective from the one in which events are customarily viewed in Synod.

Common Worship does show some signs of movement in a new direction. No longer are we invited to look forward to a time when "the old linguistic patterns" will no longer prevent a "truly critical reform".[20] The Prayer Book is to be given parity of esteem, as far as that is in the gift of the powers that be. It is possible, however, to be more positive.

"The ASB 1980 [the book that, as we saw, "enshrined the breaking of the mould of four hundred years"] was clearly conceived and brought to birth in the 1970s, and inevitably carries with it some of the assumptions of that decade."[21] With equal inevitability Common Worship was conceived and brought to birth in the 1990s and must by the same logic expect to be out of date in 2011.

The whole liturgical impulse towards the spirit of the age, from the 1960s onwards, has been an aberration. An aberration, to be sure, on a large scale, but nothing worse. It can be rectified. Just see that the sacred in our language is reliably there in the seventeenth-century work, for all to use, and the successor to Common Worship can, at least, be very much smaller. It is in fact already available, at a little over five pounds a copy.

> Furthermore [as Cranmer boasted in 1549], by this ordre, the curates shal nede none other bookes for their publique seruice, but this boke and the Bible: by the meanes whereof, the people shall not be at so great charge for bookes, as in tyme past they haue been.[22]

We do not, however, expect wholesale conversions either of the liberal establishment in the church, or of incumbents listening to their parishioners, though if the pressure is maintained it will tell. But another unmistakable fact about our age is that there are a lot of new millionaires for whom what to do with their money may be a worry detrimental to

[20] Cf. *Prayers for the New Babel*, p. 85.
[21] *The Worship of the Church*, 1991, p. 15.
[22] *The First and Second Prayer Books of King Edward the Sixth*, Everyman's Library edition now reprinted by the Prayer Book Society, p. 4.

health.[23] Even those made by the National Lottery might wonder whether they can do anything more interesting with their money than put it in trust for their descendants.

Let them endow churches! as the wealthy English have always done since the days of the heptarchy. (To be sure, the new wealthy belong to the new world and need the same change of mind. But Christians do believe in redemption, and even a few rich men may penetrate the needle's eye.) Only this time let the trust deeds be well enough drawn to prevent the liberal establishment and/or the Church Commissioners getting their hands on the endowments. Let there be a Prayer Book church in every diocese, with a resident vicar, an energetically run Sunday school, and given to what the Church Army calls "outreach", that is, bringing the unchurched people to the Lord. England has to be evangelised anew, and in the war against darkness the Prayer Book is the most effective weapon we have. But only if it is brought home to people.

For £2m you can build and endow a church and vicarage. It's peanuts to many people! This is less than is lost from the EU budget in accounting error and fraud every single day! For £100m there can be at least one such church in every diocese. Then schools can be attached, daughter churches founded like the offspring of the great Minsters of Saxon times, and the reconversion of England become a serious possibility. Millionaires sometimes like newspapers to play with, or political parties. Are there really none to rescue the Church of England?

Pending the millionaires—though they may turn up at any moment—we are left with the people in the pews,

[23] Cf. *Financial Times* first article in the Money section, 15 July 2000: "Psychologists talk of a new disease that is sweeping modern Britain: affluenza."

increasingly called upon to make good the deficiencies in the Church's budgets. As above, we should not expect too much of them. On the other hand, we are always hearing from the power brokers of the media that they are speaking for everybody, and in this regard the Liturgical Commission belongs very much to what Dean Perham calls the "new world". Those who prefer the degree of uniformity represented by the Book of Common Prayer earlier in the twentieth century (and how much was that?) are, he tells us, "probably a minority"—of, one supposes, the minority left. It would not be surprising if the dwindling band left in the pews are those who can tolerate ASB or Order One. But what evidence is there that this is in fact the case? "Most church people," says Dean Perham, "consider themselves to have been enriched by the freedom that new services have brought." Perhaps he means the same majority when he says, "Most church people do not wish to see that new world disappear." [24] But he neglects the evidence. These are straightforward statistical claims. They could be substantiated—and if not they should be dropped.

"Most church people" may well be wrong. The role of democracy in an episcopal church is surely limited. But if the Liturgical Commission and the General Synod are willing to be governed by what most of us think, would they welcome a referendum? and agree to abide by the results? even if that necessitated a return to real common worship?

[24] *Celebrate the Christian Story*, p. 4.

Contributors

H.R.H. THE PRINCE OF WALES has recently become Patron of the Prayer Book Society of England. He is the author of *A Vision of Britain: a Personal View of Architecture*, 1989, and *The People's Prince, a Collection of Major Addresses*, 1992.

The Rev'd Dr PETER MULLEN is Rector of St Michael's, Cornhill and the National Musicians' Church of St Sepulchre-without-Newgate, and Chaplain to the Stock Exchange. He was co-editor with Professor David Martin of *No Alternative: The Prayer Book Controversy* (Blackwell, 1980) and is the author of many books and articles including numerous ones in defence of the Book of Common Prayer.

A. C. CAPEY, formerly a teacher, contributed substantially to *Children and their Books* (1977), the fruits of Sheffield University research into children's reading habits. His other publications consist mainly of essays in *The Use of English*, *Universities Quarterly*, *The Gadfly* and other periodicals, where parts of his projected *Translation* vs *Paraphrase* have already appeared. Mr Capey has edited *Faith and Worship* since 1986.

ROGER HOMAN is Professor of Religious Studies at the University of Brighton. His master's degree was in Government and his doctorate in sociology. He is the author of several books and articles in the sociology of religion, research methodology, ethics and Christian aesthetics. He is an Anglo-Catholic and a licensed Reader in the diocese of Chichester.

DAVID MARTIN is author of numerous books, more especially *A General Theory of Secularization* (1978) and *Tongues of Fire* (1990)—a study of Pentecostalism in Latin America. Sometime President of the International Conference of the Sociology of Religion; also International Research Fellow at Boston University and Professor of Human Values at Southern Methodist University. Honorary Professor (Religious Studies) Lancaster University and King's College, London University. Gore Lecturer (Westminster Abbey). Emeritus Professor of Sociology, L. S. E., hon. D. Theol., Helsinki. He is an assistant non-stipendiary priest at Guildford Cathedral.

DIARMAID MACCULLOCH, after studying and lecturing in Cambridge and Bristol, is a fellow of St Cross College, Oxford, and Professor of the History of the Church at Oxford University. He is a Fellow of the Royal Historical Society and of the Society of Antiquaries of London. His books include *Suffolk and the Tudors* (1986; winner of the 1986 Whitfield Prize), *Henry VIII: Politics, Policy and Piety* (1995), *Thomas Cranmer: a Life* (1996; winner of the Whitbread Biography Prize, the James Tait Black Prize and the Duff Cooper Prize) and *Tudor Church Militant: Edward VI and the Reformation* (1999). He is currently working on *A House Divided: the European Reformation 1480–1619.*

IAN ROBINSON'S books include *Prayers for the New Babel*, a criticism of the Alternative Service Book 1980, *The Survival of English* and *The Establishment of Modern English Prose*. He is co-author with Duke Maskell of the forthcoming book *The New Idea of the University*.